IB

and Formentera

P. DELANEY
3/9/86

ApíOS

By the staff of Editions Berlitz

Library of Congress Catalog Card Number:
75-13199.

Berlitz Trademark Reg. U.S. Patent Office
and other countries – Marca Registrada.

Printed in Switzerland by Weber S.A., Bienne.

10th Printing
1984/1985 Edition

IBIZA
and Formentera

How to use our guide

- All the practical information, hints and tips that you will need before and during the trip start on page 101, with a complete rundown of contents on page 100.
- For general background, see the sections "Ibiza and Formentera", p. 6 and "A Brief History", p. 11.
- All the sights to see are listed between pages 22 and 59. Our own choice of sights most highly recommended is pinpointed by the Berlitz traveller symbol. A special chapter on Formentera begins on page 53, with a summary of practical information on page 59.
- Entertainment, nightlife and all other leisure activities are described between pages 61 and 84, while information on restaurants and cuisine is to be found on pages 84 to 93.
- Finally, there is an index at the back of the book, pages 126 to 128.

Although we make every effort to ensure the accuracy of all the information in this book, changes occur incessantly. We cannot therefore take responsibility for facts, prices, addresses and circumstances in general that are constantly subject to alteration. Our guides are updated on a regular basis as we reprint, and we are always grateful to readers who let us know of any errors, changes or serious omissions they come across.

Text: Ken Bernstein
Photography: Ken Welsh and Jürgen Klein
Layout: Doris Haldemann
We are grateful to Charles Wenham for his help in the preparation of this book. Neville Parmenter and Pat and Miguel Cassin provided us with invaluable information. Our thanks are also due to the staff of the Spanish National Tourist Office on Ibiza, particularly Ricardo Castillejo.

Cartography: Falk-Verlag, Hamburg.

Contents

Ibiza and Formentera

Ibiza is where today's tourists coexist with movie stars, con-men, artists, the last of the hippies—and islanders who sometimes wear their quaint native costumes to work. Fortunately for all concerned, the cultural shock is attenuated by the soothing sun.

First, let's scrap some misconceptions. Ibiza is *not* one of those barren Mediterranean rocks whose allure begins and ends at the beach. It is *not* so exotic that the food and drink make you groan or gasp. And although it's a part of Spain, it is *not* the usual bullfight-and-flamenco scene. The people are a race apart. They have a unique, ancient heritage and a passionate folklore all their own.

Geographically, Ibiza is nearer to the coast of North Africa than to the Catalonian metropolis of Barcelona. Its area is only 220 square miles,

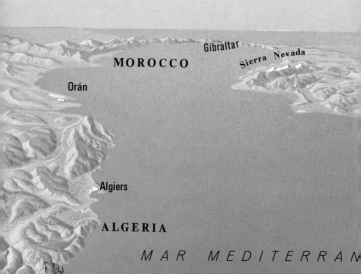

MOROCCO Gibraltar Sierra Nevada

Orán

Algiers

ALGERIA

MAR MEDITERRAN

slightly smaller than the Isle of Man or twice the size of Massachusetts' Martha's Vineyard. It's not much of a speck on the globe but big enough to contain a modest mountain, verdant farms and—that ultimate Mediterranean novelty—a river.

An hour's ferry-boat ride from Ibiza brings you to the smaller, sister island of Formentera. The ancient Greeks lumped Ibiza and Formentera together under the title *Pitiusas*—pine-covered islands. For many years, during the supremacy of the Barbary Coast pirates, Formentera was so vulnerable it had to be abandoned. It wasn't resettled until the 18th century. Ibiza is surrounded by minor islets, uninhabited but eminently explorable.

Mountain climbers won't be impressed by Ibiza's Mount Atalaya (about 1,560 feet high). But on a clear day, you can see Spain from the top.

Closer to sea level live 65,000 permanent inhabitants. During the summer season they become a harried minority in their own country.

ESPAÑA

Alicante

Valencia

Formentera   Ibiza

Palma

Cabrera

Mallorca

Barcelona

Islas Baleares

E O

Menorca

N

As advertised, the climate is gentle. Extremes are avoided. In winter it's unusual for the mercury to approach the freezing point. In summer, blistering heat is rare, and the breeze relieves the sting. But, nevertheless, the climate is tending to get hotter, and forest fires are not unknown.

The climate, complemented by extraordinary underground water resources, assures the success of Ibiza's agriculture. For the tourist, the olive, fig and almond trees are objects of beauty and colour; for the farmer, they're cash crops. So is the salt, drying as it has for centuries in the huge, square pans on the island's southern expanse. But the sounds of the traditional industries—shipbuilding, fishing, mining, sandal-making—have been all but drowned out by the clanging cash register of tourism.

One local industry in particular attracts tourists for serious but not necessarily sober investigation. Alcoholic beverages based on local herbs are commercially produced on Ibiza. These widely reputed drinks can be surprisingly mild—or just surprising.

The capital and principal city of Ibiza is called, simply but confusingly, Ibiza. Its year-round population is some 30,000. With its houses all white-washed (by official decree), the ancient walled city grows up a hillside, easily matching the charm of any other Mediterranean "jewel". Tourist interest isn't limited to the old town; it encompasses the sizeable port area with its hustle and bustle, bistros and boutiques. Trendy Ibiza Town, notorious for non conformists, also has a conventional side, thanks to its position as financial, governmental and administrative centre. An 18th-century ditty irreverently described "our regal city of Ibiza" as a clutter of "ministers and attorneys-general, judges and governors, tax and rent collectors enough to fill a hall".

The most informal and thoroughly touristic town on the island is 15 kilometres west of Ibiza. The Romans called it Portus Magnus (great port). The Ibicencos corrupted this to Portmany. Both versions are still seen in the local nomenclature but the official Spanish name of the boom town is San Antonio Abad—Abbot St. Anthony. High-rise hotels and apartment buildings have sprung up all around the breathtaking bay and have turned San Antonio into a sort of Copacabana Beach. San Antonio is a centre not only for beach activities but for swinging nightlife as well.

The second largest town on the island is Santa Eulalia del Río on the east coast. Until very recently it was just a hamlet on a hilltop crowned by a picturesque fortress-church. Now the tourist imperative has extended the town all the way down to the sea and far along the coast. The magnitude of Santa Eulalia's river shouldn't be exaggerated but it's charming nonetheless.

Prudently shaded, a village woman quietly ponders sunbathers.

Carob tree, once a lifesaver for hungry islanders, amid a flowered pastureland. In the distance: Ibiza's ancient capital city.

Other villages are far less developed. Therein lies many a delight for the enterprising tourist. Drive inland from your ultra-modern hotel to the less populous centre of the island, with hamlets consisting of not much more than a white-washed church, a general store and a bar. Buy a glass of *hierbas,* listen to the crickets, and watch the country-women in their flowing black dresses with pigtails down their backs. One of them may smile and offer you an orange, an almond or a fresh fig. Here they grow on trees.

A Brief History

Pillage and rape desolated Ibiza for centuries. But even the most notorious invaders—from Vandals to Moors to swash-buckling pirates—couldn't crush the spirit of independence of the people. The islanders have learned to take the long-range view. This may explain why today's tourist invasion evokes a long-suffering shrug of the shoulders.

When did man first set foot on Ibiza? A handful of Bronze Age relics has fostered an assumption that prehistoric settlers inhabited the island thousands of years ago. In any case, Ibiza's key location between Africa and ancient Iberia made it a logical stopover for the earliest Mediterranean navigators, such as the Phoenician traders, who called the island Ibosim. The Greeks dubbed it Ebysos, the Romans called it Ebusus and the Moors, Yebisah.

A detailed history of the island doesn't begin until it became a colony of Carthage in the seventh century B.C. The Carthaginians originally came from the area comprising present-day Lebanon. From bases in North Africa and what's now Spain they challenged the Roman empire for control of the Mediterranean region.

Not surprisingly, therefore, the Carthaginians weren't interested in Ibiza for its sun and fun; they had their eye on the island's vast salt flats. The fast-drying sea salt of Ibiza was a profitable industry. It still is.

Workaday Ibiza: production of salt has always been a vital industry.

The Carthaginians exploited another local industry—fishing. And then they cleverly utilized the famous Ibiza salt to cure Ibiza fish and export it to their country. They also mined lead—a local mineral resource which continued to be of significance up until this century. **11**

Hannibal's slingshot marksmen used ammunition from Ibiza.

The awesome troops of the Carthaginian general, Hannibal, deployed two secret weapons—elephants and leaden pellets the size of golf balls. These pellets were made on Ibiza and used in the slingshots for which the Carthaginians were renowned and feared.

The Carthaginians made more than just a commercial and military outpost of Ibiza. They seem to have considered the island a holy place, for here in great splendour they buried thousands of their citizens. The tranquil hill called Puig des Molins, within the present boundary of Ibiza Town, contains a Punic* necropolis. Under the gnarled olive trees archaeologists have uncovered a treasure-trove of statues, jewellery, pitchers, tools and coins. Ibiza Town boasts not one but two archaeological museums.

After the Romans destroyed Carthage in 146 B.C., a new era began for Ibiza. Local historians stress that Ibiza was neither conquered nor annexed by Rome. It became *confederated,* retaining remarkable autonomy. Thus, for centuries after the end of Carthaginian supremacy, the old Carthaginian traditions were allowed to continue on Ibiza alongside the new Roman ways. Meanwhile on the Iberian peninsula, too, Rome was leaving a decisive imprint with its language and culture,

12

---

* Punic comes from the Roman name for the Carthaginians.

Life and death in ancient Ibiza reflected in relics. Carthaginian statue of goddess Tanit has become symbol of the island.

its system of government and its engineering genius in the construction of roads, aqueducts and monuments.

The Romans continued to exploit Ibiza's natural resources. They exported salt from the southern end of the island and lead from the mines of San Carlos. And they extracted from shellfish a purple dye which was used for imperial cloaks. Another money-maker from Roman Ibiza: an exotic, aromatic sauce of decomposed fish innards. Called *garum,* it was considered a great delicacy by Romans and 13

Greeks alike. For today's tourist, *garum* is but a historical footnote. Local cooks use nothing more pungent than a hint of garlic.

After centuries of peace and productivity A.D. 426 marked the beginning of an era of strife, violence and destruction. Ibiza, along with the rest of what's now Spain, was invaded and sacked by the Germanic tribe of the Vandals. They occupied Ibiza and imposed their culture. The advent of the Vandals heralded centuries of often repressive foreign rule; the Vandals were succeeded by the Byzantines, Saracens, Moors and Normans—to name a few.

Except during the periods of violent interruption typical

Potter's art of clay and fire has been handed down over centuries.

of the era, the Moorish rulers were able to devote themselves to developing Ibiza's economy and agriculture. Little evidence remains of that era—ceramics in the museum, a few fortifications, a network of irrigation ditches. For the most part, the Moorish legacy to Ibiza is intangible: a few local place-names, some words in the Ibicenco dialect and an indelible influence on the island's folk music. But the Moors are perhaps most unforgettable in the dark, brooding eyes of so many islanders of our day.

The Moors were determined to carry their Islamic faith from North Africa into Europe and to this end invaded Spain itself. They even reached into France until they were beaten by the Frankish ruler Charles Martel in 732. One event during Moorish times in Ibiza lives in local legend. The island was on the receiving end of the ministrations of Pope Paschal II. To cleanse the Mediterranean of infidels and pirates, Paschal mounted what was called the Crusade of Pisa in 1113. Ibiza was a likely target but who would have expected all 500 warships of the crusade's fleet? The ensuing offensive turned into a real medieval epic: weeks of siege, battering rams, scaling towers, crusaders clambering over the bodies of their own fallen comrades to push through breaches in the defences. The islanders put up a particularly gallant show. They rallied round the Moorish viceroy, Abdul-Manzor, to repel one bloody charge after another. Finally, the besieged Ibicencos convinced their leader to admit the day was lost and hoist the white flag. The pious Pisans accepted the surrender in the customary way: they punished the bloodied islanders, dismantled what remained of the battered city wall and hauled away all the booty they could grab.

After that, Islamic domination waned, and in the early 13th century Ibiza was embraced by the Christian Reconquest. King James I of Aragon (in northeastern Spain) authorized the occupation of Ibiza and Formentera under forces commanded by Guillermo de Montgrí, a solid Catalonian citizen with titular ecclesiastical rank. Compared with the Pisans' massacre a century earlier, Montgrí's invasion was easy. After a few skirmishes, the Catalonian troops were ready to deal the death blow.

One pincer battered its way through the rebuilt city wall. The other, according to tradition, infiltrated through a secret passage revealed to the invaders by the brother of the sheik himself. Legend says the traitor gave the game away because he was embittered and

Archaeological museum in old town: a 'must' visit.

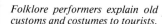

Folklore performers explain old customs and costumes to tourists.

northern Andalusia, but they still clung to the kingdom of Granada and were only finally evicted from there in 1492.

Elsewhere, great events were changing the shape of the world. Under Ferdinand and Isabella, the unity of Spain as the country we know today was finally achieved, and it was under their auspices that in 1492 Christopher Columbus sailed westwards to try to reach the spices and riches of the East and instead discovered America. This discovery —or rather re-discovery—soon brought immense wealth to Spain in the form of gold and silver. It turned the attention of Spanish rulers away from the Mediterranean and Ibiza towards the New World and also towards the heart of Europe where Spanish ambitions rapidly expanded. Ibiza became a mere backwater, forgotten but for shipwreck or plague.

As the Spanish monarchs looked the other way, the daring pirates of the North African Barbary Coast—and elsewhere—moved in. The Ibicen-

sulking; the passionate sheik had seduced his wife.

Thus, violently, in August 1235, Christianity and the Catalonian language came to Ibiza to stay.

On the mainland, the Reconquest was a bitter struggle that lasted more than five centuries. The Moors suffered a major setback in 1212 at the battle of Navas de Tolosa in

cos fortified the bulwarks and constructed additional towers and fortresses throughout the island to help shield themselves against further enemy incursions. Despite their efforts, Ibiza was menaced by so many hostile flotillas that the locals organized an original defence. They formed a sort of antipirate pirate fleet of their own, the Corsairs of Ibiza. To the Berbers' amazement, Ibiza's privateers turned the tables on them by brashly boarding their brigantines on the high seas and "liberating" the pirates' booty.

The most villainous foreign swashbuckler of all, according to local tradition, was a pirate from Gibraltar, Capt. Miguel Novelli, alias The Pope. His 250-ton pirate ship, ironically named the Felicity, deployed a dozen cannons. A local captain, Antonio Riquer, commanding a frigate one-quarter the size of the Felicity and with only eight guns, took on the arrogant pirate. The battle raged for an entire afternoon midway between Ibiza and Formentera. The total population of both islands stood along the beaches to cheer Riquer the Giant Killer. The local boy made good.

An obelisk in Ibiza's port honours the daring Corsairs.

Another reminder of the incessant pirate incursions is found in the layout of most of the island's towns. Their

On capital's most lively promenade, patriotic statue honours Joaquín Vara de Rey, local hero who died in Cuba in 1898 Spanish-American War.

churches and traditional centres of activity are elevated and inland. The idea was to provide an early warning system. Sometimes it worked.

Elsewhere on the island, last-ditch defences in the form of round stone towers were built in many isolated regions. A few are still inhabited. An unusual collection of these towers may be seen from the San Juan road in a hamlet with the Moorish name of Balafi, near the village of San Lorenzo.

In the 19th and early 20th centuries, Spain was not only

Balafi houses included towers for defence against the pirates.

economically feeble but also politically unstable. It had already lost its empire in America and the Pacific. In Morocco, too, the country suffered a humiliating defeat at the hands of local rebels in 1923. Under the last Spanish king, Alfonso XIII, neither dictatorship nor constitutional government was able to provide domestic tranquility, and in 1931 the king went into exile following anti-royalist election results.

The life of the new republic continued to be turbulent, however, with bitter ideological divisions between parties and factions and with the church also involved. Finally, in 1936, a large section of the army under Gen. Francisco Franco rose in revolt against the government. On his side were monarchists, conservatives, the Church and the right-wing Falangists. Against him was a collection of republicans, liberals, socialists, communists and anarchists.

The civil war became one of the *causes célèbres* of the 20th century with support for both sides coming from outside Spain. To many people in Europe, often unaware of or indifferent to the particular Spanish origins of the struggle, it was seen as a crucial conflict between democracy and dictatorship or, from the other side, as a conflict between law and order and the forces of social revolution and chaos. The bloodshed lasted three years and cost a million

Years of sun and hardship reflected in peasant woman's face.

lives. The tragedy touched almost every family on Ibiza as well as the mainland. As if that weren't enough, hardship continued throughout World War II.

The Spanish economy was shattered, and in the years which followed the end of the war recovery only inched forward.

The significant surge in tourism in the 1960s bolstered Ibiza's economy. And the expansion of its airport to accommodate jet aircraft signalled a welcome new invasion—this time of sunworshippers from the North.

With the death of General Franco and the advent of democracy, Ibiza's tourist industry continued to grow. So did a sense of Ibicenco identity and a new atmosphere of freedom. Gambling has been legalized and nude bathing sanctioned. Change has come to Ibiza—dramatically, irrevocably, almost overnight.

Ibiza: Facts and Figures

Geography	Third largest of the Balearic Islands, situated in the western Mediterranean Sea. Area 220 square miles, slightly smaller than the Isle of Man or twice the size of Martha's Vineyard in Massachusetts. The principal city is Ibiza Town (year-round population 30,000), followed by Santa Eulalia (13,000) and San Antonio (11,000).
Climate	Mediterranean, with mild winters and dry, sunny summers.
Population	65,000 permanent residents, swelling in season to many times more.
Government	Ibiza forms part of the Spanish province of Baleares, the capital of which is Palma de Mallorca.
Economy	Ibiza's prosperity rests almost exclusively on tourism. Traditional industries like ship-building, fishing and salt-production run a very distant second.
Language	Ibicenco, a dialect related to the Catalan language, and Spanish.
Religion	Roman Catholic

Where to Go

Once you've seen your hotel and beach it's time to go and see Ibiza. You can join a coachload of excursionists or try to figure it out for yourself in a rented car. Although it's a small island, you'll only have time to scratch the suface.

From architecture to zoology, Ibiza offers exhibits seen nowhere else on earth. Whether your interests are as serious as ancient history or as flighty as windsurfing, you'll find new stimulation on *la Isla Blanca*—the White Island, as this Balearic is often called.

Each area offers something different. The Sa Peña and Dalt Vila districts of Ibiza Town have lots of trendy boutiques, Santa Eulalia boasts some of the island's best restaurants, while San Antonio is notorious for its discos and bars. You'll also want to discover the real Ibiza—the country of farmers and fishermen. Just wander off the beaten path, beyond the densely infested tourist zone.

And if you crave a change of environment, a day's outing to Formentera offers the bonus of a sea voyage. Life is simpler on this secluded Balearic island and beaches are less crowded. You'll probably be tempted to stay put for awhile, relaxing in one of the Mediterranean's quietest corners.

Ibiza Town
Pop. 30,000

Most tourists arrive on the island by package-tour jet. Their first impression is an international terminal big enough to justify Ibiza's position as eighth busiest airport in Spain.

But don't let this vast impersonal facility mislead you. Ibiza is a relaxing fireside in a frozen world of efficiency and hygiene. Start seeing it in the capital, a gallery of history and humanity.

Most tourists guiding themselves through a sightseeing

day in Ibiza Town arrive by bus from one of the outlying resort complexes. The buses stop either at the station on Isidoro Macabich, or—in the case of the small blue buses —opposite the Delegación del Gobierno building further down the same avenue. Having survived the first blast of exhaust fumes, traffic tangle and hubbub, the worst is over. The same avenue meets Avenida Ignacio Wallis; turn to the right down it and a few hundred yards later you'll come to Paseo Vara de Rey. This modest boulevard is where the local youngsters congregate to decide what to do for the evening. On one side of the strolling area a news-stand offers an engrossing array of Europe's newspapers and magazines. In the middle of this pleasant promenade stands an old-

Finding Your Way

On Ibiza and Formentera some place names are in Ibicenco, while others retain their Spanish forms. The same goes for words like "street", "square" and "cape". The following list of key terms in Spanish and Ibicenco will help you make sense of maps and street plans and find your way around the islands more easily.

	Spanish	Ibicenco
avenue	{ avenida \ vía	{ avinguda \ via
beach	playa	platja
boulevard	paseo	passeig
bridge	puente	pont
bullring	plaza de toros	plasa de braus
cape	cabo	cala
cave	cueva	cova
church	iglesia	esglèsia
fountain	fuente	font
harbour	puerto	port
quarter	barrio	barri
river	río	riu
road	carretera	carretera
square	plaza	plasa
town hall	ayuntamiento	ajuntament

IBIZA TOWN

fashioned, rousing **monument** to one of Ibiza's few native sons to make a mark on Spanish history. The local hero, Joaquín Vara de Rey, was a Spanish general who died defending the colony of Cuba against the Americans in the war of 1898.

By mid-morning doors open wide on La Marina's cavernous shops and storerooms.

On one side of the street are some outdoor cafés where a *café con leche* can be stretched over a whole morning of basking in the sun, postcard-writing, map-reading or watching the colourful crowds. The cafés nearest the port attract the so-called Beautiful People, among others. Here the yellow tablecloths are clean, and the waiters, with great formality by local standards, wear bow-ties and white jackets. Here the town tycoons transact business in the civilized Spanish way: over sherry or brandy. And the hippies at the next table live their own fantasies, fuelled by the rays of the sun and possibly other easily obtained stimuli.

Experienced Mediterranean travellers will be pleased to note an absence of beggars. The authorities have made it known that they're unwelcome. An occasional lottery-ticket hawker may make his presence known but it's very definitely a soft-sell. The really persistent beggars are the stray dogs. They use countless ploys to endear themselves to café patrons. The dogs are as gentle as they are handsome.

After a coffee break and an eyeful of the passing crowds, it's time to begin an unpackaged tour of the town. The most logical place to start is down at the **harbour.** The port is virtually round the corner from the *paseo,* a favourite spot to stroll in the city.

An imposing pier in the centre of the dock area serves the liners from Palma, Barcelona, Valencia and other scheduled ferry points. The passenger terminal is a modern building with a restaurant on top. At any time at least one of the white ships is loading or unloading cars, cargo or passengers, so there's plenty of maritime mystique for you to savour at leisure.

In front of the terminal, now serving as a traffic roundabout, the **Corsair obelisk** *(Obelisco a los Corsarios)* is believed to be the world's only monument in praise of privateers (see HISTORY, page 17).

Inland from here is the heart of the district called **La Marina** which genuinely looks the part of a Mediterranean port. If you can disregard the souvenir shops for the moment, there are sights to remember here: women in black blending into the shadows, fishermen coming home from the sea and everywhere the traditional white houses with flower pots adorning wrought-iron balconies. Explore the hilly, narrow streets of the arm of land called **Sa Peña.** The laundry dripping dry from upper floors may splash you; children, dogs and cats may get in your way, the aromas of coffee, spices, fish and baking bread may distract you. If the senses, to say nothing of the feet, need a break, relax on the waterfront with its abundance of open-air cafés. **27**

(At night this district swings in its own far-out and boisterous way.)

A few streets back into the town from the passenger terminal and the privateers' obelisk is the inevitable Quaint Old Market. This high-roofed, open-sided **market-place** *(mercado)* is where fruit and vegetable dealers set up their stands. The morning is its busiest, most colourful time—an adventure in itself.

 Opposite the market is the principal entrance to the walled city, **Dalt Vila,** the old town of Ibiza. A ceremonial ramp leads across what used to be a moat into an impressive gateway. A Latin inscription over the arch dates the wall at 1585 in the reign of Philip II of Spain. On either side are white marble statues, headless but gracefully robed. They were unearthed on the spot during a 16th-century construction project. According to the barely decipherable Latin inscriptions, one of the statues honours a Roman senator; the other is an aristocratic Roman family's tribute to Juno, principal Roman goddess.

Other walled cities survive but Ibiza's **seven-bulwark defences** are almost completely intact. There are three ancient gates into the city. Historians say the Carthaginians initially constructed a wall here though there are no remains of it. The Moors built a second wall of which towers and remnants are still evident today. The present bulwarks date back to 1554 when Charles V, a Holy Roman emperor, ordered that the six-foot-thick wall be reconstructed. The fortifications are a prime surviving testimony to the military technology of the time. They've been proclaimed a national monument.

The tunnel through the great wall leads to a classic quadrangle fit for royal reviews. These days there's no more pomp under the porticos. Instead, a variety of artisans vie for display space to peddle their jewellery and leatherwork, often quite original and cheap. The **Patio de Armas,** arsenal square, as the quad is called, leads into the first of several wide-open plazas which surprise the visitor climbing the maze of narrow alleys. In the

Modern-day artisans sell their creations near ancient city walls.

old town of steep, cobbled streets, curious dead-ends and unexpected vistas, a map isn't really necessary. The most important directions are simply up and down. Up leads eventually to the cathedral and fortress commanding the hilltop. Down inevitably leads to

Through this wall to Dalt Vila, a medieval city within a city.

one of three gates through the wall to the new town. The variations are almost infinite. Wrong turns may be recommended, for every zigzag brings another delight—a sweep of bougainvillea, a baroque doorway, a fashionable restaurant or a new perspective on the sea and city below.

When you think you've reached the top of the town—at an impressive plaza with a 16th-century church and a whitewashed town hall—you haven't. It's only an excuse to catch your breath. Admire the view down the cliffside from the edge of the city wall, then continue on ascending the narrow streets.

Suddenly you're in another cobbled square. The **cathedral** on your right was built on the site of a Roman temple and a Moorish mosque. Construction began in the 13th century with renovation in the 16th and again in the 18th centuries. This has made for architectural eccentricities which may be interesting in themselves. Some medieval works of art are visible inside, but at a price. A museum is attached to the cathedral; tourists are asked to "donate" a few pesetas *before* they can cross the threshold of the church. A final oddity: the church is called *la catedral de Santa María de las Nieves* (Our Lady of the Snows)—an offbeat choice of a patron saint for this sunny part of the world.

Across the square is a **museum** *(Museo Arqueológico de Dalt Vila)** housing one of Ibiza's two archaeological collections. Together, they comprise one of the world's great treasuries of Carthaginian art. All the relics were discovered on the island. They range from statues and urns to priceless jewellery and coins.

Many items are self-explanatory, which is fortunate because all notations are printed in Spanish only. Keep in mind the formula for dates: *III siglo a. J.C.* means third century B.C.; *XII siglo d. J.C.* means 12th century A.D.

The museum is compact enough to cover in half an hour. If you're still in a condition to walk, try to pick your way to Portal Nou, another gateway through the great wall. You'll be deposited in the modern part of town in the middle of luxury apartment buildings, offices and shops. Only four long streets away is the **Museo Monográfico Puig des Molins***. This modern, spacious "new town" museum is built on the edge of a particularly attractive hill covered with olive trees and wild flowers. It's called **Puig des Molins**—"hill of the windmills". Here the Carthaginians, and later the Romans, buried their dead with respectful ritual. The artefacts displayed in this museum were all unearthed on the spot. Again, the inscriptions are in Spanish only. Outside, around the corner of the building, is a cavelike entrance to the necropolis itself. Several typical burial chambers have been cleared and illuminated for the tourist's inspection. In all, there are some 4,000 vaults. After you've seen the works of art which were buried with the bodies, the crypt shouldn't be too gloomy a sight. But if you need cheering up after paying your respects to the very long departed, wander to the far side of the hill for a view of the sea. Nearby is the beach of Figueretes (the little fig trees). There, the bodies, alive and warm, belong to bathing beauties of a dozen nationalities.

*See also section on galleries and museums, p. 61, and box, pp. 62–63.

31

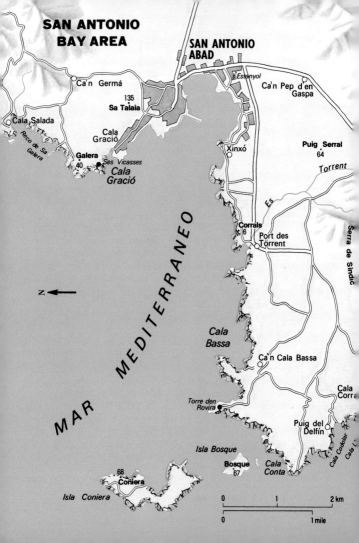

San Antonio Abad

Pop. 11,000
(Ibiza Town, 15 km.)

Until the 1960s, San Antonio was a fishing village tucked into the pine trees on one end of a magnificent bay. Nowadays the bay is cluttered with all kinds of yachts, fishing boats, sailing-boats, ferryboats, glass-bottom boats and even workaday freighters.

The town now looks like a proper Mediterranean resort of white skyscrapers. But rather than a capital or trade centre, San Antonio is the swinging heart of package-tour Ibiza. And instead of a corner of the bay, it now extends for miles. This is a problem in itself.

The newer hotels have been built on distant beaches, providing doorstep swimming and sunbathing but requiring a bus or ferryboat ride to the shopping and nightlife. If, on the other hand, you're staying at a hotel or apartment in town, you'll have to travel to find a desirable beach. Either way, the distances involved have become significant, requiring careful planning of each day's programme.

The town itself comprises a hotch-potch of modest old stucco houses and luxurious new edifices. Traditionally, activity was centred four streets up the hill from the present seafront. The **14th-century church,** white and solid, contains an attractive patio accentuating its gentle arches. Like many of Ibiza's churches, it was built as a combination house of worship and fortress.

For the tourist the centre of town tends to be the **maritime promenade** (Paseo Marítimo), a bayfront park area reclaimed from the sea in a rare act of civic virtue after the tourist boom began. The *paseo* comes equipped with trees, flowers, a fountain, benches and a proliferation of outdoor cafés.

This is where the ferryboats, mostly converted fishing boats, compete for passengers. They go to beaches near and far; usually, but not necessarily, the farther the better. Yet there's a beach for every taste. Families with children may seek the gentlest incline of sand and the least ripple of wavelets; while snorkellers may be happier with a rocky coastline which happens to attract the feeding fish. Often both kinds of swimming exist in one area.

Trial and error is a **33**

reasonable approach in this field since even the errors tend to make for a pleasant outing. All the beaches served by ferryboats or buses have snackbars, rentable beach-chairs and umbrellas and additional amenities to one degree or another. It should be mentioned that *no* Ibiza beach maintains lifeguards.

The municipal bus station is next to the bayfront promenade, virtually on the sea itself. Buses to the beaches are cheaper and faster than the ferries, if less adventurous. However, service is restricted to beaches close to San Antonio. Due to geographical and historical factors, no one has ever built a round-the-coast road. Thus many of the best beaches may be reached only by dusty trails more suitable for horses and carts than buses. But then it's luxury for some to "discover" a relatively secluded patch of beach.

Dominating the mouth of San Antonio Bay is the gaunt silhouette of the island of Coniera, or Conejera (meaning rabbit's warren or burrow). Legend calls this uninhabited island the birthplace of the great Carthaginian warrior, Hannibal. Its other claim to fame is an automatic lighthouse whose signal flashes can be seen 30 miles away.

From San Antonio, Coniera appears to be almost hopelessly inhospitable, but a tiny hidden harbour makes it possible for boats to moor. The island is

Siesta time in San Antonio: on the waterfront and under the arches of the fortress-church.

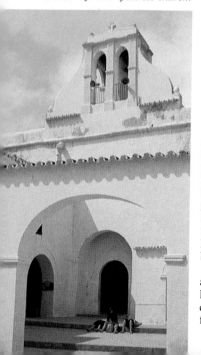

well stocked with tenacious pines, wild flowers of delightful variety and crowds of friendly, hungry lizards. The swimming is unsuitable for children. Among other perils of the deep, the area suffers an overpopulation of sea urchins whose spiny quills are such a menace to tender feet.

All the small, secondary islands attract flocks of seabirds.

Back at San Antonio, the waterfront itself provides a pleasant sightseeing stroll. At the imposing, modern jetty there's a dreamworthy fleet of sailing-boats and motor yachts to gawk at. Some are designed for the daring, others for the cocktails-on-the-poopdeck crowd. There's no law against staring; in fact, it's a common Spanish trait.

Santa Eulalia del Río
Pop. 13,000
(Ibiza Town, 15 km.)

Tourists arriving in Santa Eulalia may be forgiven if they wander about looking for the centre of town. It's not at the top of the hill, where a medieval fortress-church makes a pretty picture against the blue sky. It's not at the seafront, a rambling, confused and sometimes unappealing stretch of cove.

If the island's second largest town has any centre at all, it's the sleepy square in front of the sagging old police barracks. The monument in the tiny plaza recalls a shipwreck of 1913. A fountain on the far side of the square features jets of water spurting from the mouths of bizarre fish statues. **35**

Across the main road is the start of a boulevard laid out in the style of Barcelona's gracious *Ramblas*. But in tiny Santa Eulalia the effect is somewhat muted. The tree-lined avenue extends less than three blocks to the sea.

Santa Eulalia was the first Ibiza village to attract foreign visitors—decades before the invention of the package tour. A significant, and in some cases notorious, colony of foreign artists and writers has grown up, scattered through the district around Santa Eulalia. The tourist must give these expatriates credit for at least one achievement: they inspired an uncommon variety of good restaurants and interesting bars.

In the past, Santa Eulalia was primarily a market centre for the rich farms of the northeastern quadrant of the island. Now it has become the shopping centre for tourists based as far up and down the coast as es Canar and Cala Llonga. Both resort areas are linked to Santa Eulalia by bus and ferry-boat.

For the casual tourist the only "must" in the village is the old **white church** on the hilltop, surrounded by the cube-shaped houses which distinguish Ibicenco architecture. The ensemble looks different from each direction and at various times of day. It has inspired a hundred different artists and every amateur photographer within range. Some of the old houses on the hilltop are admirably

decorated with flower gardens. All have a panoramic view of sea or mountains—or both.

From the top of Puig den Missa you can look down onto Santa Eulalia's noted "river" (a trickle, in fact) and two bridges spanning it. The modern one, just wide enough for two cars to pass, parallels a low foot-bridge of apparent Roman construction. Island legend claims the low bridge was built in one furious night by the Devil himself. If you're not too superstitious, wander down to the old cobbled bridge and cross into a quieter world.

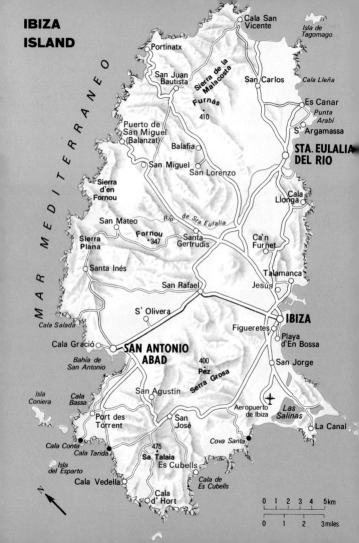

Inland on an Island

Two roads connect Ibiza Town with San Antonio. The shorter route goes through SAN RAFAEL, a village whose white church is relatively modern but stately in a Spanish colonial way. A sightseeing bonus: from the plaza in front of the church there's an unexpectedly stirring aerial view of Ibiza Town. Some orange groves sprawl enroute on both sides of the Ibiza—San Rafael road, and the parched landscape is attractive. But don't let your eyes stray from the business of driving for long. Traffic can be heavy on Ibiza's main east-west thoroughfare, and drivers somewhat capricious. Watch out for cars passing illegally and other potential dangers.

The more circuitous road between Ibiza and San Antonio passes in sight of SAN AGUSTÍN. There's not much to the village, though the site is attractive. You may want to visit the church, the most prominent structure around. Walk to the rear door and rouse the priest, who lives at the back in stoical underemployment. He'll open the entrance to the sanctuary and leave you to inspect the blue and white tiles on the walls, the Baroque-style altar and his own tiny kitchen beyond. Have a look, too, at the round defence tower across the road, converted for use as a family dwelling.

Further along, you come to SAN JOSÉ, a village known for its handicrafts. Several shops sell local embroidery and souvenirs.

Not far from San José, just off the highway, is **Cova Santa** ("holy cave"). Unfortunately, nobody seems to known how it got its name. Whatever the story, this privately owned cave, of modest proportions, is open to tourists for a small fee.

Another side-trip along the

Accent on the Vernacular

Ibicenco, the dialect the islanders speak among themselves, is a subdivision of the easten branch of the Catalan language.

It sounds rather like Portuguese. Its roots are Latin, and its vocabulary is spiced with Arabic ingredients. But don't worry, nearly everyone knows Spanish too.

The name of the island can be mispronounced any number of ways. The correct Spanish pronunciation is ee-BEE-tha.

San José road leads to **Mount Atalaya** (referred to locally as sa Talaia), highest point on the island. A chancy road winding up to the 1,560-foot summit will test the engine and suspension of your rented car as well as your own persistence. The view of Ibiza, the sea and the Spanish mainland is predictably inspiring. Three quarters of the way to the summit,

Altar triptych in 15th-century church in village of Jesús.

Ses Roques Altes ("the high rocks") was the scene of the island's most devastating tragedy of modern times. In 1972 a chartered airliner crashed here in fog, killing more than 100 people, nearly all Ibicencos. A cemetery was established on the spot.

Back to the touristical pursuit of villages which retain the old traditions: a short drive or a hefty hike north of Ibiza Town is the village of JESÚS. The **15th-century church** here looks particularly moody. Like many of the rural churches, it's often closed and locked just when you might like to look inside. If you're lucky enough to gain entry, you'll see the only major work of art on the whole island: the **Gothic triptych,** or altar retable, which is attributed to the artist Rodrigo de Osona.

Indeed most of the churches of Ibiza are worth a visit for their architectural, historical or scenic merits. Notice the black crosses painted on the white walls of houses near a church, reminders of the devotional stations of the cross celebrated on Good Friday.

The medieval church of SAN JORGE, a few miles southwest of Ibiza Town, combines spacious, gracious arches with no nonsense bulwarks for its defence. On the northern side of the island, the 14th-century **church of San Miguel** affords a hilltop view of the distant sea. The cruciform edifice is graced with fresco decorations in black and white. In the church-yard is a fascinating collection of antiques including a wine press and a grain mill. The church's ample patio is taken over regularly for folklore exhibitions in which a group of dancers perform to the vigorous accompaniment of traditional instruments (see pp. 76–78).

Houses are rather sparse from here across the fertile valley to the sea. Some of them have their own built-in baking ovens which are still used daily. The artistic arrangement of cobblestone and brick on the floor of some barns is worth a peek.

You may want to visit a few of the other inland hamlets —Santa Inés, San Juan, San Carlos, for example. Each has the ubiquitous historic church, bar-restaurant and shop or two. Villagers generally welcome tourists, viewing them with a fair amount of friendly curiosity.

While You're Wandering...

The rewards of a close-up look at the countryside of Ibiza include a botanical treasury. If you're interested in plants and flowers, here's a calendar:

January:
mimosa bushes covered with yellow puff-balls.

February:
white and pink *almond* blossoms, unforgettable as a blizzard; and on the hills giant blue *iris, yellow gorse* and tiny *bee orchids.*

March–April:
fields of *daisies*—even daisy bushes—and pink *field gladioli* announce spring on Ibiza.

May–June:
the striking scarlet of flowering *pomegranate* trees contrasts with the red of *poppies* in the corn fields and the bright yellow flowers of the *prickly pear.*

July–August:
now the garden flowers bloom: *honeysuckle* in yellow and cream; the blue, trumpet-shaped *morning glory* and pink and white *oleander; bougainvillea* starts to sprout

42

bright green leaves and scarlet flowers; by the beach the white, sweet-scented *sea daffodil* pushes up out of the sand.

September:
rainbows of *geraniums, petunias, dahlias;* and see the white spikes of the *yucca plant.*

October:
zinnias, brown and yellow; the *prickly pear* bears egg-sized fruit of yellow and purple; tiny *narcissus* and *merendera* flower after the first autumn rains.

November:
in shady woods, white and pink *heather* hugs the ground; *rosemary* bushes, covered with tiny blue flowers, dot open areas.

December:
orange and *lemon trees* bear fruit.

And almost year-round in the most unexpected places— in tiny crevices between rocks, alongside every road and path —the wild flowers, sometimes almost microscopic, offer a kaleidoscope of colour and life.

From top to bottom: page 42, fig marigold, poinsettia, morning glory; page 43, aquilegia, borage, anacamptis.

43

Thick whitewashed walls protect country houses from summer heat. Architects laud the concept of an expandable cluster of rooms.

Witches and Whitewash

Superstitious country folk carry on elements of pagan witchcraft. In many Ibicenco hamlets, old women credited with supernatural powers treat ailing people and animals. These witch doctors use incantations and herbal medicines.

Another tradition says certain bottles contain *diablillos,* little devils or imps. If a housewife opens the bottle improperly she is plagued by all manner of minor domestic problems.

Some tourists are also hexed by bottles, but that's a demon of another colour.

Every springtime, the hardy women of Ibiza whitewash their houses. They do it eagerly—with almost religious enthusiasm. There's a suspicion among some anthropologists that the whitewash craze may derive from some remote Punic ritual. Local poet Fajarnes Cardona termed it, "That whiteness, an exorcism of all that's sordid".

Architects from abroad point out that each house represents a conjunciton of one-room units, infinitely expandable to suit conditions. Instead of the traditional patio, Ibiza has opted for open verandahs with stately arches. Triangular-topped chimneys, outside staircases and cubist tendencies have inspired modern architects near and far.

Ibiza's Dogs and Lizards

Ibiza claims a unique zoological attraction, the celebrated Ibicenco hound. Skinny as a greyhound, long-snouted with alert big ears and eyes as mysterious as a Siamese cat's, this hungry-looking dog can trace its history back thousands of years. But for all that, it's said to be less intelligent than most common mongrels.

No dangerous animals, poisonous insects or plants imperil natives or visitors to Ibiza. And the only reptiles are harmless lizards, of which there are two dozen varieties. These descendants of the dinosaur abound, sunning themselves on rocks or foraging among pine cones. Rarely more than six inches from tongue to tail, they're no more dangerous than butterflies. Another species of lizard may be found in your hotel, possibly clinging to the ceiling. Don't disturb. These fellows are mosquito catchers.

The usual barnyard animals can be seen on your excursions across the island. Cattle-raising isn't important. If they're not foraging in the orchards, dark brown pigs will be found in muddy sties where they're fattened on the island's prickly pears.

Birdwatchers will enjoy classifying a variety of species, while canaries, finches and parakeets cheerfully sing away in birdcages hung outside the windows of Ibicenco homes.

Ibiza's famous hound was depicted in ancient Egyptian drawings. **45**

Busy coastal waters: a boat is often the fastest way to a beach.

Circumnavigation

If you've a boat and plenty of time to explore Ibiza's 106 miles of coastline, so much the better. If not, this survey covers seaside places more or less easily accessible by land. Let's start at the top of the compass and work our way clockwise round the island. And note again that in the absence of a coastal road, you usually have to go far inland every time you want to travel from one beach to another.

The northernmost tourist centre is PORTINATX (pronounced port-ee-NATCH). To get there from the fertile farmland of the centre of the island you drive over substantial hills,

alongside cliffs and finally down to an unexpectedly placid sea. The natural beauty of the area—sandy beaches, weird rock formations and plenty of juniper and pine trees—hasn't escaped the hotel and villa promoters. Local boosters won't let you overlook two historical claims to fame. In 1929, during Spanish naval manoeuvers off Ibiza, King Alfonso XIII came ashore here. Immediately, the name of the place was officially changed to Portinatx del Rey ("of the king"). More recently, part of the film "South Pacific" was shot on the beach at Portinatx.

Clockwise from Portinatx, the next major point of interest is CALA SAN VICENTE. While

Excursion boats now link uninhabited Tagomago to Ibiza.

exceptionally hilly and circuitous, the road is good enough to handle a stream of tourist buses. This splendid cove is now a centre of characterless modern hotels with villas climbing steeply from there. They all enjoy a precious view, but the beach itself is likely to be overcrowded. Up in the hills behind SAN VICENTE—a rough hike over difficult terrain—is a cave called **es Cuieram.** Considerable archaeological treasure was found here on the grounds of an ancient temple dedicated to the Carthaginian goddess Tanit (see pp. 62–63). Most of the artefacts can be viewed at the archaeological museum in Dalt Vila. The cave is now just a good place

to seek temporary shelter from the hot, midday sun.

Much of the coastline south from Cala San Vicente is good, sandy beach. Areas served by roads are being built up and tend to be crowded at the height of summer. You have to wander farther afield to find open space, peace and quiet, to say nothing of seclusion on the sand.

Almost directly offshore from here is the island of TAGOMAGO, now linked to the ''mainland'' of Ibiza by regular excursion boats. Although the beach at Tagomago is too narrow for sunbathing, the swimming is superb. It's worth the trouble to ramble up to the extraordinary lighthouse at the **47** top of the hill past abandoned farms, wild flowers and great sea vistas.

Es Canar, the official Ibicenco spelling for a variously mis-spelt beach, has become a major tourist centre. It now sprawls along several beaches. Tourist-oriented nightlife is abundant here. There's a popular weekly hippy market in nearby Punta Arabí. Special bus services run from Santa Eulalia, and agencies programme excursions to it. Beware of cheap gold watches— and of pickpockets.

Hikers may want to try the

Sunbathers stake out their corner of paradise. Beaches more remote than this one lack umbrellas, deck-chairs and other amenities.

coastal path from es Canar all the way to Santa Eulalia and beyond. It follows piney coves, mysterious cliffs and quiet beaches. A beach bar's refreshment is never far away.

CALA LLONGA, south of Santa Eulalia, is what its name says—a long cove. From some vantage points it looks like a Norwegian fjord. Hotels and apartment construction now push back into the hills. Locals and day trippers from Santa Eulalia pack the deep, sandy beach.

Cala Llonga's worst problems are a thing of the past. Pollution, once rampant, has now been halted by the construction of a sewage plant some distance away.

An impressive rocky coastline with a backdrop of verdant hills continues southward to TALAMANCA, a heavily built-up beach with a fine view of Ibiza Town. On the other side of the capital is FIGUERETES, a hotel complex, and then the long, straight sea-front beach of PLAYA D'EN BOSSA. Along here occurred a notorious back-to-the-drawing-board incident. A 600-room luxury hotel had to be demolished just as it was ready to open for business. It had mistakenly been built directly on the flight path to Ibiza airport.

At the southern extremity of the island, near the salt flats, are some hard-to-reach, mostly unspoiled beaches. Among them is PLAYA CABALLET, officially reserved for nude bathing. Other nearby attrac-

Far from a world of traffic jams, a gentle, flowered place to stroll.

tions include the quarrying operation itself and the salt-exporting port called LA CANAL. The sprawling salt flats—nearly 1,000 acres at or just below sea level—have a fascination of their own. The white mountains of dry salt, the shimmering patterns on the heavy water, make it a sort of Dead Sea outpost in an otherwise green and hospitable land. Some 60,000 tons of salt a year are harvested here.

More sand or rock beaches continue westward from LAS SALINAS, but they become less and less accessible. The scenery is more spectacular towards the southwest corner of the island. The hamlet of Es CUBELLS, reached by road from San José, sits in a land's-end position overlooking rocks and a blue sea. A theological seminary is idyllically perched above the rocky crest.

The western side of the island, leading up toward San Antonio Bay, comes under the jurisdiction of San José. It includes some of the finest beaches on the island—or anywhere in the Mediterranean for that matter.

Aficionados dispute the merits of CALA BASSA, CALA VEDELLA, CALA TARIDA and CALA CONTA, but each has something very special to offer. At these coves, bathers enjoy crystal-clear, clean water and splendid, gently sloping beaches. There are good road connections between San Antonio and both Cala Tarida and Cala Vedella, with the result that both bays are on their way to becoming rather built up. You can also reach Cala Bassa and Cala Conta by road (there's a bus service), or by boat. The combination of red and greyish rocks, the white sands, the green pines and the rich blue sky and sea is striking. The caves nearby have become a playground for the local Tom Sawyers.

Once past the small coves north of San Antonio, the rest of the coastal circle is something of a no-man's land of cruel rocks and relatively fierce seas. No real road leads to the coast in this whole quadrant, with one major exception. The beach called PUERTO DE SAN MIGUEL, a narrow inlet far below and beyond the hilltop town of San Miguel, used to have the Moorish name of Balanzat. Now one side of the inlet has been given over to an outburst of sleekly modern hotels. Fortunately, tourists staying in these air-conditioned palaces have their own swimming pools, for San Miguel beach couldn't comfortably accommodate them all at once.

The most popular local attraction is **Cova de Can Marça,** a cave where light and sound effects enhance the natural wonders of stalagmites and stalactites.

If overexploitation has changed the face of Ibiza's coast, thus far the unblemished areas overwhelmingly outnumber the pock-marks. A tourist who never leaves the beaten track will, alas, never know.

Like most market-places, this one in Ibiza Town's Sa Peña district deals in news as well as produce.

Formentera

Less than four nautical miles separate Formentera from Ibiza. The people and the language are the same. Yet the two islands couldn't be farther removed. Formentera has no airport, nor are there any plans to build one. A ferry service provides the only inter-island link. The Balearic outpost boasts a sizeable salt lake but no fresh water. Cisterns, some of them dating from Moorish times, catch whatever rain falls from the sky—with supplementary water supplies shipped in as required.

Not that developers haven't made inroads here. Hotel complexes and scores of apartment blocks line the beaches of es Pujols, Mitjorn, es Caló and Cala Sahona. These centres attract most of the tourists and summer residents, who swell the permanent population of around 4,500 to 20,000 or more. The impact of this seasonal influx of tourists (mainly German, British and French) has been dramatic but not overwhelming. There's still room to spare on Formentera.

Constrained by the limited water supply and lack of an airport, the pace of construction and change is kept within reasonable bounds. Buildings may not rise higher than four storeys, so there are no skyscrapers to mar the landscape. The island has also avoided an explosion of automobiles. Bicycles and, to a lesser extent, mopeds prove the favoured means of tourist transport: an estimated 8 to 10,000 bikes are available for hire. There's no better way to get around on an island that measures no more than 12 miles from end to end—one-fifth the size of Ibiza.

Day-trippers in a hurry scramble onto tour buses for a fast look at the sights, an activity that *can* be accomplished in record time. But most visitors prefer to linger in Formentera. They're attracted by the sun and sea, by the incomparable beaches and some of the best windsurfing and scuba-diving in the Mediterranean. Sandy beaches like Playa Mitjorn go on for miles. Here and elsewhere, you'll see many nude sunbathers, and toplessness is the order of the day. So far nude bathing has been legalized only on the **53** isolated beaches of Illetas and Levante, but it is practised virtually everywhere. As a rule, officials take no notice.

For all Formentera's freewheeling ways, traditions remain firmly entrenched. Farmers prosper as precariously as ever, scratching a living from the arid, rocky soil. Wheat, barley and oats are the most significant crops, wheat having been cultivated since Roman times, when the island was known as Frumenteria or "wheat-producer". Vineyards provide grapes for Formentera's distinctive dry red wine, *vino pagés*. Almond and fig trees thrive, but the olives bear little fruit.

Life still revolves around stuccoed farmhouses with tiled roofs and columned verandahs. Lush red tomatoes, threaded in garlands, hang from the rafters to dry. Almonds are shelled for sale to tourists, together with honey, figs and the fruit of a winter's knitting: pullovers, caps, scarves and socks fashioned from the coarse, cream-coloured local wool. Islanders seem reluctant to abandon a rural lifestyle, however enthusiastically they welcome tourism.

The surf's up along Playa de Mitjorn's five-mile expanse.

Island Sights

From Ibiza Town, ferries depart punctually for the port of LA SABINA, a journey of around one hour. The route passes in sight of two uninhabited islands: ES VEDRÀ, which hovers like an apparition on the horizon off to the west, and ESPALMADOR, popu-

lar with yachtsmen for its white sand beach. Small but sturdy craft make the crossing, more often than not carrying a full complement of passengers. They disembark onto the quayside, taking in at a glance the languorous activity of the harbour and the spate of new construction that is changing the skyline of La Sabina. Here you can rent a car, bike or moped, or catch the bus. La Sabina serves as the terminus for Formentera's limited public transport system, and there are taxis available for hire.

Follow the main road inland, past the island's lone petrol station (closed after dark!), to the town of **San Francisco Javier.** The population of Formentera's chief city has expanded to nearly 900, and there is a new town hall. Parked at the back is the jaunty landrover that serves as a fire engine, the first on Formentera—and just one beneficial side effect of the tourist boom. Another is the land-rover *cum* ambulance and the municipal health centre. But the most prominent structure in San Francisco is its **18th-century church.** This fortress of whitewashed stone, squat as a bunker, sheltered townsfolk when pirate raids threatened. Now tourists descend on the town's three main streets, and a growing number of souvenir shops proclaim the new order of things.

From San Francisco, take the road that leads southwest to Cabo Barberiá (southernmost point in the Balearic Islands). Just over a mile out of town, you pass the turning to CALA SAHONA, a small sandy bay. Framing it are cliffs of red rock, where stand a hotel and holiday apartment blocks. Except for Cala Sahona, this part of the island is sparsely populated. There are a few farms, scattered fields marked by stone walls and corrals enclosing sheep, goats and pigs. The parched landscape grows ever more desolate as you approach CABO BARBERIÁ, and the road deteriorates until it's no more than a dusty track. The cape itself is the haunt of wild goats and the site of an isolated lighthouse and a watchtower, built high above the sea.

After the solitary beauty of Cabo Barberiá comes **Playa de Mitjorn,** a sublime arc of sand five miles long, popular with holiday-makers in the summer season. The area has been developed with several hotels, notably Club Hotel La Mola, Formentera's most luxurious resort, Hotel Formentera Playa and the Mar-y-land complex. Continue east to the village of NUESTRA SEÑORA DEL PILAR and on to **Faro de la Mola,** an old lighthouse built in 1861 and still in operation. A veteran keeper lives on the premises, tending the beacon that is visible 40 miles out to sea. Faro de la Mola figures in the Jules Verne adventure *Journey Round the Solar System,* a fact commemorated by a monument nearby. Though time and technological advances have passed the lighthouse by, it's not difficult to see why it caught Verne's imagination. Literary connections apart, the site has a certain splendour, affording as it does ravishing views over Formentera and out across the wind-tossed sea.

Negras · Isla de Ahorcados

Faro d'en Pou

I. Torretas

Espardell · Isla Espardell
27

Isla Espalmador

Playa de Illetas

MAR

I. Ponet
I. Redonda
Moll Marroig
Las Salinas
Playa de Levante
Playa d'es Pujols
Punta Prima

nta
Pedrera
LA SABINA
Estany
Es Pujols

MEDITERRÁNEO

Pudent

Torre de
La Gavina
a'n Jaime
Paret
Ca'n Plater
Ca'n
Bertomeu
56
San Fernando

SAN FRANCISCO
JAVIER
Las Rocas
Ca'n Serra
Ca'n Pep
Blau

la Sahona
Ca'n Fita
Can Xiquet
Tavé
Ca'n
Mayans
Camp

Punta Rasa
Torre des
Pi des Catalá
Es Caló
Can
Campanitx
Na Sa
del Pilar

Playa de Mitjorn

107
Guillem
Punta de S'Anguila
Mola 192
Ca'n
Mayans
Faro de
la Mola

Club Mar-y-land
Club La Mota

Es Plá del Rey

Torre des Cap

Cabo Barbería

N

0 1 2 3 4 5 km

0   1   2   3 miles

FORMENTERA
ISLAND

More glorious still is the panorama from the **mirador** above es Caló, one of the highest spots on the island. You can't miss the lookout point: it stands right alongside the road in full view of the narrow spine of land that connects eastern Formentera to the western half of the island. The white expanse of Playa de Mitjorn is clearly visible on the southern side, paralleled by the rocky strip of beach on the **es Caló** side. Es Caló's tiny harbour dates back to Roman times, when it was Formentera's only port. Nowadays it is a target for tourist development, and there are several small hotels and apartment complexes set in the pine woods.

After es Caló, return along the main trans-island road to SAN FERNANDO, a pleasant village with a picturesque church.

From San Fernando, take the road that heads back to the coast at **es Pujols,** Formentera's premier resort village. Scores of bars, restaurants and kiosks cater for all the tourists, many of whom are German. Not surprisingly, the beach is awash in lounge chairs and sunbaked bodies, pedalos and windsurfing gear.

Further west there are some less populous stretches where you can swim in relative seclusion or eat at an unpretentious beach restaurant. Don't expect much in the way of facilities; these simple establishments are supposed to be dismantled at the end of every season.

The oldest construction on Formentera—a **dolmen** or prehistoric stone circle—lies not far from es Pujols at Ca Na Costa (between the La Sabina road and Formentera's salt lake). Although it is still under excavation, you can visit the site. A shelter has been erected to protect the limestone monoliths from the elements. Also in the area are Formentera's salt pans, **Las Salinas,** which yield 20,000 tons of salt a year. The salt has large crystals which are considered excellent for curing fish. The export point is, of course, La Sabina —first and last port of call on this round-island jaunt.

Formentera Briefing

Ferry Service. Travel to Formentera is by ferryboat only. The 11-mile trip from Ibiza Town to the port of La Sabina takes just over one hour. Service is frequent in the tourist season, with reduced but regular sailings in the winter months. The journey can sometimes be rough. Note that departures keep to published timetables.

Bus service. One vehicle—bright orange and impossible to miss— shuttles between La Sabina, San Francisco, San Fernando, es Pujols and La Mola. The schedule coordinates with ferry arrivals and departures.

Car hire. The makes available on Formentera are those best suited for local driving conditions. Purchase fuel and oil at the petrol station outside La Sabina on the San Francisco Javier road, the only one on the island. As a rule it opens daily except Sundays and holidays until dusk.

Nude bathing. The beaches of Illetas and Levante, to the north of La Sabina, have officially been set aside for nude bathing, and the practice has spread to many other areas as well. Generally, islanders and police cast a blind eye.

Telephone. Since there is no telephone office on the island, both local and long distance calls have to be made from a hotel or public call box.

What to Do

Galleries and Museums

Archaeological museums. The **Museo Arqueológico de Dalt Vila,** at the top of the walled old town of Ibiza, exhibits finds from all over the island (especially terracottas and fertility figures from outlying sanctuaries and necropolises), plus a selection of Roman and Arabic artefacts. The **Museo Monográfico Puig des Molins** in Vía Romana displays articles discovered in the Carthaginian necropolis nearby: scarabs, unguent jars, jewellery, mirrors and razors—even highly ornate sarcophagus handles. But the richest trove of all is the superb collection of terracottas. Be sure to take a look at the powerfully modelled series of goddesses, imperial in their elaborate necklaces, gold nose rings and earrings. While you're on the spot, you may want to visit the necropolis proper, where several burial chambers are open to view. The largest of them, from six to fifteen feet deep, held several sarcophagi and a whole array of funerary furniture.

Cathedral Museum, adjacent to Ibiza's cathedral at the summit of the old town; obligatory "donation" at the door; contains municipal and church memorabilia. The star item in the collection is a monstrance (receptacle for the host) from Majorca. This prized example of medieval silverware probably dates from the late 15th century.

Museum of Modern Art, *Sala de Armas* (arsenal) alongside the city wall, just inside the old town; one-man shows and group exhibitions in a venerable setting.

Art galleries. These are found in Ibiza Town and on the road to San José and San Miguel, as well as in San Antonio and Santa Eulalia. Special shows are advertised. The island attracts artists of all styles and levels of expertise. The sheer volume of their output is prodigious.

Hotels and bars. Ibiza's artists also display their works in many tourist hotels and expatriate bars. If you're a collector, look for price tags or ask the hotel desk-clerk or barman. **61**

Ibiza, Colony of Carthage

Ibiza was swept into the orbit of Carthage in the 7th century B.C. From the time of its colonization by the North African nation, the island steadily grew in importance and for centuries it ranked as one of the major commercial and military centres in the Mediterranean. Decline set in with the defeat of Carthage by the Romans (146 B.C.). Yet Ibiza held fast to the fierce gods and gory customs of the Punic past, preserving the traditions of Carthage long into the Roman period.

Archaeologists paint a fascinating picture of life, death and ritual in the Punic colony. More than 20 ancient sites—necropolises, or vast cities of the dead, and religious shrines—have been explored since the turn of the century. And a wealth of objects (jewellery, metalwork and ceramics) has come to light. The most important necropolis, at Puig des Molins, boasts some 4,000 tombs, though less than 300 have actually been uncovered. Here you can see the spacious burial chambers constructed for rich citizens of the Punic capital. They were laid to rest in enormous stone sarcophagi, surrounded by the paraphernalia of a happy afterlife: unguent jars, lanterns, terracotta statuettes of deities, ostrich eggs decorated with symbols of life and resurrection. The less affluent made do with a shallow tomb or simple sarcophagus set into the hillside. Cheaper still, if less roomy, was an ordinary amphora just large enough to hold the ashes of the departed.

Apart from its funerary function, Puig des Molins may have been the scene of infant sacrifice. There was also a pottery near by, in what is now Vía Romana. This is where all those terracotta figures of gods and goddesses were made. Most of them were formed in clay moulds and baked in a wood-fired oven, though some were modelled by hand and others turned on the wheel. The statuettes probably represent deities who protected the dead in the next world. Of special significance for the Carthaginians were Tanit, goddess of the underworld, and her consort Baal.

In the Punic colony, the art of the potter was handed down from father to son. There were plenty of craftsmen with a repertoire to match: figurines of animals associated with Tanit (the lion) and Baal (the bull); clay plaques with the image of Death as a horseman or various life-and-resurrection symbols, especially palm branches, lotus flowers and the crescent moon; fat fertility goddesses; statuettes of worshippers and so on. Striking in their simplicity, these pieces follow North African prototypes. They are coarse and unsophisticated—made for a people whose business instincts were more highly developed than their aesthetic sensibilities.

Other important Punic sites include the sanctuaries of Isla Plana, a little peninsula jutting into the Bahía de Ibiza, and es Cuieram, a cave near San Vicente in the sparsely populated northeastern quadrant of the island. From the earliest period of Carthaginian colonization, Isla Plana was a holy place. People came here to seek protection against evil in general, difficulties in childbirth and childhood illnesses in particular, even death itself. Es Cuieram was dedicated to the cult of Tanit, at its peak from the 4th to the 2nd centuries B.C. The isolation of the cave did not stop believers from depositing gold medallions and hundreds upon hundreds of terracotta figures here. Oddly, nearly all the terracottas were blackened by fire, and this, together with the quantities of bones and ashes uncovered in the cave, points to the performance of some kind of funerary rite at es Cuieram.

For all its vitality, Punic culture died out. By the close of the Roman era, es Cuieram, Isla Plana, Puig des Molins and Ibiza's other sanctuaries and necropolises lay abandoned and forgotten. But not for long. After the Arab conquest, thieves plundered the tombs of Puig des Molins, stripping them of precious gold jewellery. To complete the archaeological record, they left behind the lamps that lighted up their search.

Sadly, the plunder continued early this century, when unscrupulous archaeologists formed private collections of Punic art and artefacts in the course of "official" excavations. There were plenty of clandestine digs, too. One antique dealer from Mallorca kept a legion of islanders on the lookout for additions to his collection. He later exhibited his finds in Barcelona, pocketing the proceeds. Not long afterwards, Barcelona's archaeological museum acquired every last object for a handsome sum.

Although many key pieces of Punic art have been dispersed or lost, many more are on display in Ibiza's archaeological museums. Gold work, jewellery, the painted spheres of ostrich eggs and exquisitely modelled terracottas—all provide valuable insights into the island's past. These objects of ritual and ornamentation perplex and intrigue; they sum up as nothing can the spirit of Carthage itself.

Sports and Outdoor Activities

With year-round sunshine and the Mediterranean lapping at its shores, Ibiza is ideal for aquatic sports. While the emphasis is on swimming and sailing, you may prefer to do nothing more strenuous than lie in the sun and become an amateur spectator.

Formentera, for its part, boasts some of the most beautiful sandy beaches in the Balearics, and the scuba-diving and windsurfing can't be bettered.

One important cautionary note: the summer sun wreaks havoc with the unwary. As Sir Noel Coward so succinctly put it, only mad dogs and Englishmen go out in the midday sun. Leave it to the mad dogs. In the beginning, half-hour sunbaths in the morning and late afternoon will create the groundwork for a good tan. Even when you've grown ac-

Fool around with a beach ball or make waves off Formentera in a catamaran-for-hire.

customed to the rays, wear a tee-shirt or something light over your shoulders. And a hat is a good idea, too. Don't be complacent even in winter. Northern noses have been seen to peel under the November or March sun.

For an idea of the cost of various sports, consult the PLANNING YOUR BUDGET section on page 99.

Boating and Sailing

Very few holidaymakers arrive in their own boats or are otherwise self-sufficient for sailing. But don't worry. Plenty of beaches have sailing-boats for hire. The rates are about the same as in mainland Spanish resorts and sometimes cheaper.

According to Spanish law, only captains with an official licence can operate motor-boats. The law is strictly enforced, and as a result motor-boats are seldom available to tourists.

Sailing-Boats. Suitable for a crew of two, these are just the ticket for learning to sail. Beach bars and most water sports schools rent out sailing-boats. At schools tuition is optional.

Pedalos. These two-seaters

ply the seas powered by a foot-driven water-wheel. They're stable enough for a young child to be aboard accompanied by an adult, perfect as a personalized ferry-boat to snorkelling coves or just to avoid the crowds. Pedalos can be hired by the hour, and you should allow yourself plenty of time to return to shore before your time has expired.

Rowing-boats. Not too common on Ibiza's beaches, but occasionally rentable.

Windsurfing

Windsurfing is becoming increasingly popular on Ibiza and Formentera; equipment can be hired at "escuelas de windsurfing" and certain resorts. This sport more or less takes the place of water-skiing, which is rarely practised now.

Fishing

Fishing along the rocks of the coastline is a popular pursuit, however elusive the prospect of a big catch. Offshore, the professional fishing business, once a major island industry, has dwindled significantly. These days, island fishmongers are just as likely to sell frozen fish from far afield as the freshly caught local article. Some dawdling fishermen work the banks of Ibiza's Río de la Santa Eulalia, especially at the point where it empties into the sea. But don't expect too much more than a nibble. However, fun and success can be had "spinning" from the back of a boat; catches of brill up to a foot long are commonplace in winter. The equipment is readily available and very cheap.

Scuba-Diving

First of all, fishing with scuba equipment and gun is absolutely forbidden. Secondly, the shores of Ibiza contain so much archaeological treasure that the government keeps a sharp eye on all divers. Before you can go under water you need a licence from CRIS *(Centro de Recuperación y Investigaciones Submarinas—* Underwater Recovery and Research Centre). The authorities take this most seriously, and violators may be prosecuted.

But all is not lost. Scuba-diving schools operate on Ibiza and Formentera, though the locations tend to change from year to year. You must apply yourself for a licence;

a medical certificate is also required.

Fortunately, the whole family can enjoy a hint of the thrills of undersea swimming. Snorkelling equipment is quite cheap in the shops but test the face-mask carefully before you buy it. With a little practice almost anyone can flip off to an interesting rock formation and watch the multicoloured fish pass in review. Snorkelfishing with spearguns is quite legal. The fish, often frisky with unarmed snorkellers, have learned to scatter at the sight of a harpoon.

If you don't feel squeamish about it, you can prowl the rocks in shallow waters with face-mask and spear in search of squid. These tentacled creatures look monstrous under water, but once out in the air they're revealed as small and not dangerous. In winter, thousands of squid lurk amongst the rocks in very shallow waters along the coast, and the only equipment needed to catch them is a face-mask and *gancho* (hook). The problem is learning to differentiate between the squid and the rocks they settle in. If you can solve that one you'll have

a lot of fun. Everyone in sight will congratulate you, as well as advising you how to cook and eat your catch. Need a recipe? The simplest method is to simmer the squid in its own ink. Otherwise hang it up on a line until the sun completely dries it out (at least 12 hours), cut it up into very thin slices, grill it over open coals, and then sprinkle it with lemon juice. Delicious. Or so the locals say! For something along the same lines but not quite so esoteric, try a dish of *calamares,* or deep-fried squid, in a local restaurant.

Swimming

Your hotel pool, a deck-chair-strewn beach or a secluded cove—take your pick.

Most Ibiza hotels and apartment complexes have their own freshwater swimming pools with all conveniences, tempting guests not to wander. On Formentera, however, this is not the rule.

Amenities inevitably go together with crowds, so on the main beaches be prepared to do battle with jet-loads of other sun-seekers, all equally happy that restaurants, toilets, showers and changing rooms **67** are close at hand. Territorial rights, in the form of a deck-chair, can be assured for a nominal sum.

The concept of a professional life-guard is unknown on Ibiza and Formentera alike. Some beach-bars keep first-aid supplies. Happily, most of the favourite beaches are well protected from waves and undertow and slope gradually. Normally they couldn't be safer, but on a rough day, take care!

If you're willing to leave the

The clear, cool waters of the Mediterranean are perfect for snorkelling, scuba-diving and plain old paddling. There's plenty of scope for the tennis buff, too.

beaten track you can still find cliff-backed coves with clear, blue water or patches of sand scarcely large enough for two families.

Conscious of adverse criticism, the authorities have begun taking measures to clean the beaches. Legislation has been introduced to discourage ships from spilling oil off the coast.

Tennis

Although there are no grass courts on the islands, a number of asphalt or composition courts are available at hotels and apartment complexes.

Courts can be hired by the hour. You may have to book ahead. A few hotels have professionals on the staff who'll give you lessons. Prices vary greatly according to the reputation of the teacher.

Whether you take your tennis seriously or just like to hit a ball around, be careful of the midday sun. New arrivals especially should lie low during the most blistering hours to avoid burns or exhaustion.

Hunting and Shooting

Which came first, the famous Ibicenco hounds or the island

craze for weekend hunting forays?

In either case, the locals go into the hills for the exercise more than for the kill. Rabbits and an occasional partridge are about the extent of the possibilities. The season runs from October to February. Clay pigeon shooting is popular, too.

Check for details on hunt-

Between swims, golfers make a bee-line for Cala Llonga, while shoppers search for souvenirs.

ing permits with a Spanish government tourist office or write to I.C.O.N.A., Carrer Sabino de Arana, 22, Barcelona.

Golf

One unexpected sight, in a remote valley near Cala Llonga, is a civilized, meticulously tended, exquisitely green golf course. Visitors to Ibiza are welcome to tee off.

Archery

Adepts with bow and arrow can practise their favourite sport on Ibiza and Formentera.

Minigolf

If you can't get into the golf club scene, try minigolf in San Antonio, Santa Eulalia or Portinatx (Ibiza). Club La Mola on Formentera provides minigolf facilities for their guests.

Horseriding

The countryside of Ibiza, with its gentle green hills and grid of back roads, lends itself to riding. There are stables in Santa Gertrudis, Portinatx, San Antonio and near Santa Eulalia. Instruction and children's mounts are also available.

Riding is a good way to see the offbeat side of Ibiza so often missed by tourists—the unspoiled interior of the island where life is almost as simple as it ever was.

Shopping

Shopping Hours

Ibiza's shopping hours are from about 9 a.m. to 1 p.m. and from 4 to 8 p.m. In summer some shops remain open an extra half hour or more in the evening to cope with the crush.

Bars and cafés are generally open from as early as 8 a.m. until midnight or later with no break for the siesta.

Most boutiques open only during the tourist season from Easter till November.

Best Buys

As a rule, prices on Ibiza are higher than on the Spanish peninsula and there are few real bargains these days. Ordinary shoes, both men's and wo-

men's can be quite cheap, but anything stylish is likely to cost as much as at home. Traditional *alparagatas*—shoes of straw and hemp and other ingenious, indigenous materials—are just the ticket for beach outings, shopping trips or lounging around the hotel, bungalow or outdoor café. Even though they're not very practical to wear when you return home, they're cheap enough to buy and forget.

The straw bags which Ibicencos and visitors hang over their shoulders for shopping or for carrying beach equipment are useful and inexpensive. They come in several sizes—for children and adults, for carrying odds and ends or for buying out the supermarket. To keep up with tourist demand, the local supply

of authentic, handmade baskets is augmented with imported goods.

Jewellery of gold and silver made on the spot or elsewhere in Spain proves popular for both quality and price. You'll also see hippy-made jewellery on sale, especially at the market in Punta Arabí. The artisans themselves look like a replay of the sixties.

There's nothing like the trendy resort clothing available here, styled on the island by designers of the Ad Lib group. They're renowned as far away as New York for their Ibiza look. In another category altogether are the hand-knitted and crocheted articles made by island women.

Locally produced pottery may also interest you. The terracotta bowls have centuries of tradition behind them; the ashtrays are also attractive, if less authentic. But inadequately fired, unglazed pottery is risky to ship or pack.

Liquor and tobacco are cheap—by European' and American standards. Prices in town are low, while those at the airport duty-free shop are lower still. Imported Cuban cigars—plentiful and cheap —are a favourite take-home present—though they're still outlawed by U.S. customs. While foreign-brand alcohol, produced under licence in Spain, goes for only a few hundred pesetas a bottle, there are more unusual local spirits which might make more apt souvenirs of Ibiza. These drinks are flavoured with Ibiza's wild herbs, resulting in interesting and varied flavours. *Hierbas, anís seco, anís dulce, frigola* are just a few names.

Another shopping note: herbs and spices, bought off the shelf in local supermarkets, cost very little. Take home a bunch of tiny packets of *azafrán* (saffron) and any other dried herbs you may fancy. An overpoweringly fragrant shop in the port area of Ibiza Town stocks just about every spice known to Western civilization.

A variety of local and Spanish foodstuffs can be transported home with a minimum of fuss and bother: olives, olive oil, almonds, dried figs, cheese, sausage. Look for these items in Sa Peña's picturesque little open-air mar-

Hand-painted plates and tiles: new twist in ancient handicraft.

ket (Ibiza Town) or—for a wide selection—the bustling, covered central market in the newer part of town (Calle de Extremadura).

Souvenirs

With so many millions of foreign tourists on holiday in Spain—and so many of them "repeat" visitors—the souvenir industry is hard-pressed to devise novelties annually.

If you insist on buying "traditional" Spanish souvenirs, there's no shortage of shops overflowing with mock bullfighter swords from Toledo, inlaid Moorish-style chess sets, imitation antique pistols, bullfight posters (with or without your own name imprinted as a star toreador), statuettes of Don Quixote, wrought-iron novelties and the typical Spanish *bota,* the soft leather wineskin (which is likely to be lined with plastic these days).

But don't fool yourself. These trinkets have no more connection with Ibiza than plastic models of the Eiffel Tower made in Japan.

Antiques

Years ago there must have been intriguing opportunities to buy up Ibicenco antiques and ship them home. Nowadays it would take more days of scrounging about than the average tourist is willing to invest. But browse around in the shops. If they haven't already boosted the prices beyond all reason, you may find an appealing piece of old ironwork or hand carving. At the least you can always take home a rusty old door key or two suitable for haunted houses or a kitchen iron of genuine pre-electric vintage.

Where to Shop

The area around the port in Ibiza Town provides the largest selection of shops on the island. Quite a few devote themselves primarily to local customers, rather than tourist extravagances. Here, too, are all the boutiques that outfit Ibiza's trendier visitors.

Shopping Tips

It's always wise to price items in more than one shop before deciding what and where to

74

Everything but the kitchen sink fits into an Ibiza basket.

buy, as prices tend to vary from shop to shop.

Occasionally, you'll see a notice of sales—*rebajas*—in shop windows. While legitimate sales do take place, usually at the end of the season to dispose of unsold stock, you'll have to be a bit cautious. What seems to be a special bargain price for "one week only" could turn out to be a year-round tourist trap. Here, too, shopping around is the best way to know a bargain when and if you see one. Haggling is now a thing of the past.

Entertainment

Folklore of Ibiza
The truly local art form, found nowhere else, is Ibicenco folkloric singing and dancing. Regular shows take place in some villages, such as San Miguel; at fiesta time in other towns and villages there are often additional performances.

First, a note about the lavish costumes: the men wear red hats similar to the Catalonian model, bandannas round the neck, gold-trimmed black cor-

duroy or cotton jackets over their loose-fitting white shirts; bright red cummerbunds; baggy, white linen trousers, wide at the thighs but tight at the ankles, and the familiar Ibicenco straw shoes.

The women's costume is more complex. It includes a long, pleated skirt of black or white homespun wool; an apron with complicated patterns; a finesilk, long-tasselled shawl over the shoulders; and a big lace mantilla over the

Bottoms Up

In the Balearics, wine and water are imbibed from a communal container of glass or pottery known as a *porrón*. With its wide mouth and long, tapering spout, it looks more like a watering can than a drinking vessel. You fill it at the top and drink from the spout; the stylized shape is traditional.

Workmen carry water in a pottery *porrón,* while the glass version is usually reserved for wine. Legend credits the Moors with its invention. They were inspired, so the story goes, by the Prophet's dictum that wine should not touch Muslim lips.

The technique of drinking from a *porrón* isn't easy to master: tilt it until the liquid flows into your mouth in a stream. And don't touch the spout with your lips or tongue. Only a virtuoso manages to aim, pour and swallow at the same time— without spilling a drop.

Marching to the beat of a different drummer.

head, with hair braided down the back, sometimes tied by a schoolgirl ribbon. Around her neck she wears various strands of gold, a heavy golden necklace, ribbons, a gold scapular with images of saints on both sides and a crucifix. In addition, she wears a number of heavy rings. The costumes are so original and elaborate that a fair amount of time is spent at each folklore show explaining them in detail.

Likewise the meaning of each dance is recounted, though this is never easy when the origins have been forgotten. Most of the dances suggest ancient courtship rituals. The man is forceful and arrogant, the woman shyly flirtatious. In one dance, women form a circle, moving in small steps, their eyes cast down, while men perform high kicks keeping to the outside. Often the songs have witty, ribald lyrics likely to suffer fatally in impromptu translation.

The music is played on typically Catalonian—and in some cases uniquely Ibicenco—instruments: a wooden flute and a small drum (handled simultaneously by one ambidextrous man), a sort of steel sabre struck in rhythm and large castanets. The music appears to have survived basically from the Moorish culture, though over the centuries it has accumulated some extraneous elements. Some of the light-hearted songs require the singer to emit a weird, guttural "ye-ye-ye".

If you make your own way to the villages, it costs less than if you take an organized excursion, which includes the inevitable libation of *sangría* or local wine.

Festivals

The popular *fiestas* of Ibiza are much less pretentious than the famous *ferias* of mainland Spain. With the tourist market in mind, a few feast days have been spiced with special events and fireworks which never figured in the traditional programme when Ibiza was an unspoiled island of fisherfolk and farmers. The most interesting observances for the visitor are the modest old standbys—generally the saint's day of a village: sombre religious processions, often by candlelight; folk music; a rash of quaint costumes. It's not exactly the carnival you may have expected but much more memorable.

Principal Fiestas

First Sunday in May	Fiesta in Santa Eulalia, combining a spring festival with a flower show
June 23, 24	Fireworks, bonfires and festivities for St. John the Baptist's Day in Ibiza Town and San Antonio; this is a most important holiday for all Ibicencos. Every June 24 the landowners and tenant farmers make their verbal contracts for the coming year
July 16	Ibiza Town, festival in honour of St. Carmen, regattas; following Sunday, more of the same in San Antonio
July 25	Formentera: fiesta of St. James with procession, folk songs, dancing
Aug. 4–8	Ibiza Town honours the town's patron saint, Our Lady of the Snows, with marching bands, fireworks, folk dances, sporting events and religious services
Aug. 24	San Antonio's turn again, with St. Bartholomew's Day commemorated by a procession, high mass, concerts, fireworks and sporting events

Nightlife

Ibiza's **discotheques**—the island has over 30—attract holidaying celebrities from the cinema and entertainment worlds, as well of course as virtually every other visitor to the area.

Lots of people come to Ibiza expressly for all the discos, which run the gamut from plush to sleazy. The undisputed centre of the disco scene is San Antonio, where establishments tend to be on the brash side. In one Ibiza disco or other you can participate in activities like the nomination of "Miss Disco Queen", "Miss Sexy", "Miss Topless" and so on nightly till sunrise. Formentera can't compete with such goings on, but the island does have several discos to its credit.

Casino. Ibiza's casino, situated on the Paseo Marítimo, is open all year round. To gain entrance to the gaming room, you have to present your passport or identity papers. For a small fee, you'll be issued a computerized admission card, good for one or more days of roulette (American and French), blackjack, craps.

Stakes for many of the games are low, so you can try your hand without risking too much. Early in the evening, tourists crowd in for a look at the action, but as the night wears on, dyed-in-the-wool gamblers come to the fore.

Also on the premises are a nightclub with floor show and an art gallery featuring changing exhibits of contemporary art.

Most **films** in Ibiza's cinemas have been dubbed into Spanish. In any language, you'll hear precious little of the dialogue due to the unbelievable noise level of the chatting, whistling, footstamping audience. Aside from the more conventional cinemas of Ibiza Town, other places showing films on the island are old-fashioned if not picturesque. The wild-west-style cinema in Santa Eulalia sternly warns that it's "strictly forbidden to

Toiling in the service of tourism, Ibiza's stalwart beasts bear up under a new burden.

bring unshelled nuts into the auditorium; violators will be expelled". Once or twice a week you can now see films in English in Santa Eulalia and in San Antonio.

Donkey Treks

More than 50 trained donkeys work at the *burro* ranch near Santa Gertrudis. The outing includes a 20-minute ride over a mountain, followed by a wine-tasting party. One of the donkeys drinks *sangría* from a *porrón,* quite a feat. Tourists enjoy the scenery, the less-than-ideally-comfortable ride and the fun and games. Travel agencies sell this as an all-in excursion, door-to-door ser-vice included. If you drive to Santa Gertrudis yourself, it costs you about half as much.

Tourist-oriented donkeys are a recent development. *Burros* have been used as beasts of burden since the times of the ancient Egyptians. Those big-eared, sure-footed creatures can still be found on farms all over Ibiza, very gain-fully employed in spite of competition from tractors and trucks.

Barbecues

A popular excursion organized by tour agencies—and a fairly foolproof way of making new friends—is the all-you-can-eat-and-drink barbecue outing. Busloads of tourists are taken to a rustic setting where meat is sizzling over glowing coals. Unlimited quantities of red wine or *sangría* whet appetites. Afterwards, a band usually plays music for dancing.

You'll learn to drink wine from a *porrón,* a glass container with a pointed spout from which the liquid arcs through the air into your open mouth—theoretically, anyway. Don't wear your best clothes (see box, p. 77).

Barbecue outings represent the organized side of an Ibiza holiday.

The Bullfight

For many visitors, Spain is symbolized by the *fiesta brava,* the bullfight. Although Ibiza is in many ways distinctly un-Spanish, the island does have its own modest bullring. However, fights here are rarely top-notch; the bulls are usually lightweight and, rather than matadors, the fighters generally prove to be *novilleros,* or novices, making the rounds of the provinces. (The bullring is alternatively used for "bloodless bullfights" with audience participation, plus folklore shows and occasional pop-music concerts.)

If you've never had the opportunity to see a real bullfight, this may be your chance. You can, at least, test your reaction to the national spectacle and decide whether or not you're a potential *aficionado.*

Understand from the beginning that bullfighting isn't a sport. A sport is contest between two equals; bullfighting is certainly not that because the odds are weighted heavily against the bull.

The fight is divided into *tercios,* or thirds, each act designed to further tire the bull in preparation for its death. First the bull charges into the ring, and assistants play him with capes so that the matador can examine the way he moves, the way he prefers to thrust with his horns. Then the matador takes over and tries the bull himself, using the big red and yellow *capote.*

The second *tercio* is when the picador, the mounted spearman, lances the bull's huge shoulder muscles. This spearing has two purposes: it tires the bull, and it forces him to drop his head into a position which will allow the matador to plunge his sword between the bull's shoulder. The audience invariably boos the picador, not for any love of the bull, but simply because if the spear is used too much the bull will lose his strength and will to fight. After the picador it's the turn of the *banderilleros,* who place darts in the bull's shoulders. They're designed to counter any preference the animal may have for hooking with the left or right horn.

Finally comes the last *tercio* when the matador taunts the bull with the small, dark red *muleta,* or cape. Gradually, he dominates the bull—even to

83

the point where he can turn his back and walk away. The high point of the fight is the time which is known in English as "the moment of truth". With the bull now theoretically completely under control, the matador lunges with his sword, leaning dangerously over the bull's horns, aiming for a pinpoint thrust into a minute area between the shoulder blades which should kill the bull within seconds.

Depending upon the quality and bravery of the matador's performance, the *corrida's presidente* will indicate whether or not he is to be awarded an ear, two ears or, after an exceptional performance, the tail.

Ibiza's modern 4,000-seat arena is easy to find, only a few streets northwest of the port area. Seats in the sun *(sol)* cost considerably less than the more popular places in the shade *(sombra)*.

Beginners would do well to choose a seat in a high row to retain some remoteness from intimate details of the bullfight. No matter where you sit, it's wise to invest in a few extra pesetas in a cushion. Otherwise, it could be a long, hard afternoon.

Wining and Dining

Eating and drinking in a new part of the world can be a pleasurable adventure. It's somewhat more so on Ibiza because of a few little cultural clashes. The cook may be from Valencia, the cuisine advertised as "French" and the customers may want nothing more daring than a steak.

In the tourist hotels the food tends to be a bland, international compromise. But if you venture beyond the resort enclaves, you'll be able to sample authentic Spanish fare. Make for Ibiza Town, where *tapas* bars serve typical snacks and sandwiches to a mostly local clientele. Or explore the Santa Eulalia area, renowned among Ibicencos for its eating houses. (On Formentera, have a meal at a simple beach restaurant.)

Eating well is a passion with Spaniards. You're not likely to go wrong if you ask local people to recommend their favourite bars and restaurants*.

---

*For a comprehensive menu reader, ask your bookshop for the Berlitz Spanish–English / English–Spanish pocket dictionary or the Berlitz EUROPEAN MENU READER.

Following are some specialities:

Gazpacho (gath-PAT-cho) is an invention of Andalusia, a chilled, highly flavoured soup to which chopped tomatoes, peppers, cucumbers, onions and sippets (croutons) are added to taste. It's been described as "liquid salad" and can be a rousing refresher.

Paella (pronounced pie-ALE-ya) originated in Valencia, just across the sea from Ibiza. It's named after the iron pan in which the saffron rice is cooked. Among the additional ingredients: morsels of squid and shrimp, mussels, chicken or rabbit, sausage, peppers, onions, peas and beans, tomatoes, garlic and whatever else inspires the cook at the moment.

Paella, authentically, is served only at lunchtime and always cooked to order. It takes more than half an hour,

Confusion à la carte

Here are some menu-reading mixups to watch for:

Atún means tunny (tuna) but *aceituna* means olive.

Pavo means turkey; *pato* means duck.

Cebollas are onions; *callos* are tripe.

And if a waiter comes to your table and asks, "Menú?" it means, "Do you wish to order the special dish of the day?" If you want to study the menu to choose your meal, ask for "la carta, por favor".

time enough to pacify your hunger with another national speciality: *tortilla española,* or Spanish omelet. Unlike a French-style omelet, this one resembles a substantial egg-and-potato pie.

Since Ibiza is an island in the Mediterranean, fish figures most importantly and delectably in the local diet. Consult your waiter. If *pez espada* (swordfish) has just been hauled ashore, he'll proudly recommend a satisfying grilled steak of it. Or *mero* (grouper), *lenguado* (sole) or *salmonete* (red mullet).

Fish is usually grilled and served with a salad and fried potatoes.

In season you can find delicious varieties of shellfish —*langostinos* (Dublin Bay prawns), *gambas* (prawns) and *mejillones* (mussels).

And don't neglect *calamares,* strips of squid, most commonly fried in batter *(a la romana)*—a snack or a meal in itself.

There's plenty of meat on the menu as well: local pork and lamb, fowl and game. If you prefer a beefsteak, you'll have to choose from a confusing list of *tornedos, entrecôte* and *chateaubriand.* The most tender cut, similar to fillet mignon, is called *solomillo (filete).*

Farmyard to Table

Unlike the plasticized versions to which most supermarket clients are accustomed, the farm-fresh produce of Ibiza will jolt your palate awake.

After a large lunch on a hot day, try a bunch of grapes from the nearby vines, cooling in a bowl of water. Or a fat, juicy peach. Or a ripe melon.

In season, tourists abandon their calory fixations to dig into fresh strawberries and cream *(fresas con nata),* widely advertised by the island's restaurants and cafés.

Living on the land: tomatoes dry in garlands on the verandah of a Formentera farmstead. Wheat, oats and barley are widely cultivated on the island, and fig and almond trees thrive.

Ibicenco Dishes

Sofrit pagés: hearty meat-and-potato stew, cooked with saffron, garlic, sweet pepper, cinnamon and cloves.

Sopas: in any fourth-class restaurant you'll find a good, cheap, local soup—lentils, rice, butter beans, green beans —whatever may be at hand. If available, try *sopa de pescado* (fish soup) or *sopa marinera* (seafood soup). The rest of the meal may be just so-so but the robust opener is almost bound to be a winner.

Garbanzos: whole chickpeas served in a distinctive Ibicenco way—with parsley, oil and garlic.

Dulces: sweets, the great Ibiza weakness; from breakfast sweet rolls *(ensaimadas)* typical of the Baleares to *graixonera,* a kind of bread pudding, and *flaó,* a tart containing fresh goat cheese and mint. Even *macarrones de San*

Juan turn out to be noodles cooked in sweetened milk flavoured with cinnamon. By the way, if you come across a menu offering *filete de pescado a la romana con patatas fritas,* don't blame the restaurant for putting on airs. It's the correct Spanish way to describe fish and chips!

Restaurants

Spanish restaurants are officially graded by forks. One fork is the lowest grade; four forks the élite. But ratings are awarded according to the facilities available, not the quality of the food. Many forks on the door guarantee higher prices but not much else.

In Ibiza's old town, "dining out" really means dining out.

As good a way as any of choosing a restaurant is to look in and check how many Ibicencos and deeply tanned expatriates are eating there. If a lot of these knowledgeable, value-conscious customers congregate, chances are you'll get a satisfying meal regardless of the official rating.

Spanish restaurants sometimes offer a "day's special" *(menú del día)*. This is normally three courses plus wine at a set price. The *menú* proves economical if not inspired, since the law stipulates that the price charged cannot be more than 80 per cent of the sum of its parts.

Most menu prices include taxes and a service charge. But it's customary to leave a tip if you were served satisfactorily. Five per cent is acceptable; 10 per cent is generous.

All restaurants, for the record, announce that official complaint forms are available to dissatisfied clients.

On the Spanish mainland, late dining hours perplex visitors. Lunch never seems to start till tea-time, and dinner may wait till 10 p.m. However, Ibiza's farmer-and-fisherman tradition rules out late meals. Restaurants serve lunch from 1 to 3 p.m. and dinner from about 8 to 11 p.m.

One hint for keeping costs down. Order *vino de la casa* (house wine). It'll cost well under half the price of a brand wine with tolerable quality into the bargain.

Beach Restaurants
For drinks and snacks at the water's edge, there's nothing like a beach restaurant. These modest establishments are set up right on the sand. Because they're supposed to be dismantled at the end of each season, most of them tend to be rather makeshift. Beach restaurants are convenient and strong on atmosphere. Those on Formentera often serve cooked meals in addition to snacks, but the situation may change with the stricter enforcing of official regulations.

Bars and Cafés
From early morning to late at night these institutions serve breakfast and snacks, coffee and drinks, to tourists killing time or workers in a hurry. Open-air cafés are one of the area's pleasures. A cup of coffee buys you a ringside seat for as long as you care to dawdle; no one will rush you 89

to leave. The sole exception is in San Antonio, where some tourist-trap cafés refuse to serve coffee at all during peak hours, preferring the high profits from alcohol.

Wines and spirits are served at all hours in Spain. Children are welcome in most bars. If you see young children accompanying their families on late-night outings, don't fret; they've had a long siesta.

Bar and café bills include service, but small tips are the custom. It usually costs 20 per cent less to sit at the bar for coffee or a drink rather than being served at a table.

Note that *cafeterías* aren't self-service restaurants, but glorified snack-bars. The word originally meant a café but service has been expanded to include full meals at substantial prices.

Bodegas are wine-cellars. On the Spanish mainland, many popular tourist bars have been designed to create the atmosphere of wine cellars. However, on Ibiza, a *bodega* is usually a wholesale and retail wine store rather than a place to sit and sample the vintages. Fortunately, there's no shortage of interesting bars for that purpose.

"Foreign" Restaurants

Thanks to the tourist traffic, as well as the noted permanent colony of sophisticated foreigners, the variety of restaurants is exceptional. French, Italian, Scandinavian—even Chinese cooking—is available. The food's often quite good, though usually expensive.

Tapas

A *tapa* is a bite-sized morsel of food—meatballs, olives, fried-fish titbits, shellfish, vegetable salad; it can be almost anything edible. The word *tapa* means "lid" and comes from the old custom of giving a bite of food with a drink, the food being served on a saucer sitting on top of the glass like a lid. Nowadays, sadly, the custom of giving away the *tapa* is all but nonexistent. But the idea of selling snacks is stronger than ever. Some bars specialize in them. Instead of sitting down to a formal meal in a restaurant you can wander into a *tapa* bar, point to the items you like and eat your way down the counter, rather like a smorgasbord. Vocabulary: *una tapa* is the bite-sized portion; *una ración* is a small helping; and *una porción* is a large plate-full.

Caution: it's quite possible to spend more for a meal of *tapas* than for a good, conventional dinner.

Wines and Spirits

The most famous of all Spanish wines is sherry *(vino de Jerez),* a wine fortified with brandy. There are two main types: *fino* and *oloroso. Fino* refers to a dry sherry, pale in colour with a rich bouquet. In this category belong the *manzanillas* and *amontillados.* Any *fino* makes a good aperitif. An *oloroso,* on the other hand, is a dessert wine, heavy and dark, which is sweetened before being sold. *Brown* and *cream* sherries are *olorosos.* So is an *amoroso* though it's medium dry and pale in colour. An *oloroso* is a good after-dinner drink for those who want a change.

For a perfectly adequate table wine, try one of the many unpretentious wines that come from the mainland of Spain or Majorca. These unsung, yet worthy, vintages often cost little more than bottled mineral water. In contrast, some of the well-known Spanish wines are overpriced and not necessarily of better quality.

On rare occasions you may find a restaurant serving *vino pagés* (local red wine). Islanders often drink the somewhat acid wine mixed with lemonade *(gaseosa).*

If you're not in the mood for wine with your meal, have no qualms about ordering something else instead. No one will turn up a snobbish nose if you prefer beer, a soft drink or mineral water. At lunchtime many Spaniards consider wine off-limits—just too relaxing.

Spanish brandy has a less delicate taste than French cognac. You may find it too heavy or sweet for your taste. But it's very cheap—often the same price as a soft drink. An expensive brand like Carlos I is much smoother.

Sangría, rather like punch, is a popular tourist drink in summer. It's a mixture of red wine, lemon and orange juice, brandy, mineral water, ice and slices of fruit. If you order it with a meal, you may find it too heavy and strong. Make certain it's freshly made, not out of a bottle. Spaniards drink it as a refresher.

A word about prices. If you insist on drinking imported Scotch or Bourbon, expect to pay a relative fortune. How- **91**

Open-air café: vital institution from morning coffee to last brandy.

ever, an enormous range of familiar liquors and liqueurs are available at very low prices made under licence in Spain. A visit to a large liquor store can be an eye-popping experience; the prices are startlingly below what you'd pay at home.

Ibiza is mildly famous for its own native liqueurs. You owe it to yourself to sample some during your visit. The most common is *hierbas* (meaning, literally, herbs). This sweet and fairly mild potion is mostly a home-made product blended with herbs and sold in old bottles. The farther from tourist areas you go, the less it costs, and often the better it tastes. The syrupy *hierbas* (pronounced YAIR-bass) may be sipped before or after meals. In hot weather, the locals drink it with ice.

Frigola, a sweet, digestive drink good with ice, is commercially bottled in Ibiza from formulas requiring island-grown herbs. Two aromatic aniseed drinks are locally produced. But beware: these colourless liquids have a considerable kick. *Anís dulce* is sweet; *anís seco* is dry and dangerously potent. It quite resembles French *pastis,* Greek *ouzo* or Turkish *raki.* Ibizans like their *anís* neat (straight). Foreign imbibers usually prefer to dilute it with a large splash of water. *Palo,* a slightly bitter aniseed drink that's dark brown in colour,

tastes best with the addition of gin or soda and ice.

Breakfast, Anyone?

In Spain, breakfast is such an insignificant meal it scarcely deserves mention in our food-and-drink section.

While lunch and dinner are major meals, the standard Ibizan breakfast is only a cup of coffee and pastry. *Ensaimadas,* sweet rolls made with lard, are a Balearic speciality generally available on Ibiza. In winter you can sample *churros,* sugared fritters, that you dip into coffee or hot chocolate.

In deference to foreign habits, most hotels and some cafés now offer a *desayuno completo* consisting of orange juice, toast and coffee with or without eggs.

Breakfast coffee *(café con leche)* is half coffee, half hot milk.

To Help You Order...

Could we have a table?   ¿Nos puede dar una mesa?
Do you have a set menu?   ¿Tiene un menú del día?

I'd like a/an/some...   Quisiera...

beer	**una cerveza**	milk	**leche**
bread	**pan**	mineral water	**agua mineral**
coffee	**un café**	napkin	**una servilleta**
cutlery	**los cubiertos**	salad	**una ensalada**
fish	**pescado**	sandwich	**un bocadillo**
fruit	**fruta** ·	sugar	**azúcar**
glass	**un vaso**	tea	**un té**
meat	**carne**	(iced) water	**agua (fresca)**
menu	**la carta**	wine	**vino**

...and Read the Menu

albóndigas	meatballs	**langostino**	Dublin Bay praw
almejas	baby clams	**lenguado**	sole
anchoas	anchovies	**manzana**	apple
anguilas	baby eels	**mariscos**	shellfish
arroz	rice	**mejillones**	mussels
atún	tunny (tuna)	**melocotón**	peach
bacalao	codfish	**merluza**	hake
besugo	sea bream	**naranja**	orange
boquerones	fresh anchovies	**pescadilla**	whiting
caballa	mackerel	**pez espada**	swordfish
calamares	squid	**pimiento**	green pepper
cerdo	pork	**piña**	pineapple
chorizo	a spicy pork	**plátano**	banana
	sausage	**pollo**	chicken
cordero	lamb	**postre**	dessert
dorada	sea-bass	**pulpo**	octopus
entremeses	hors-d'oeuvre	**queso**	cheese
filete	fillet	**salchichón**	salami
fresas	strawberries	**sandía**	watermelon
gambas	prawns	**ternera**	veal or beef
helado	ice-cream	**tortilla**	omelet
huevos	eggs	**trucha**	trout
94 langosta	spiny lobster	**uvas**	grapes

How to Get There

If the choice of ways to go is bewildering, the complexity of fares and regulations can be downright stupefying. A reliable travel agent, up to date on the latest zigs and zags, can suggest which plan is best for your timetable and budget.

From Great Britain

BY AIR: Direct scheduled flights operate daily from London in the high season (April through October); flying time is about 3 hours. In the low season, travel is via Barcelona or Palma (4 hours).

Freedom fares offer savings to those who stay one day to one month, provided the return journey is not made before the Sunday following the day of departure. These fares are ideal if you want to visit several destinations in Spain. Reservations can be changed and stopovers are permitted. **Budget fares** for stays of one to 13 weeks in one destination only (no stopovers, no changes in reservations permitted) are available throughout the year. You must travel out and back on the same day of the week. A 50 per cent discount on Budget and Freedom fares is made for children age two through 11. Ask about low "add-on" fares to provincial airports in Great Britain. There are also special low season **money saver flights** for stays of between one and four weeks (no discount for children).

Fly and Drive packages, with the use of a car on Ibiza included in the price of the air fare, can be obtained with both the Budget and Freedom fares.

Charter Flights and Package Tours (including flight, hotel and board) are the most popular ways of visiting Ibiza. British travel agents offer guarantees in case of bankruptcy or cancellation by the hotels or airlines. Most recommend insurance, too, for tourists who are forced to cancel because of illness or accident.

BY ROAD: During the summer, when ferry space is at a premium, be sure you have a firm reservation. Here's how you can go:

By car ferry: the principal routes link Dover and Folkestone with Calais. Boulogne and Dunkirk; also Newhaven–Dieppe, Weymouth–Cherbourg, Southampton–Le Havre, Southampton–Cherbourg; Plymouth–Roscoff and Rosslare, Ireland with Le Havre and Cherbourg; Cork, Ireland with Roscoff.

The **hovercraft** from Ramsgate or Dover to Calais or Boulogne takes about 35 minutes and costs around the same price as the ferry.

Once in France, British motorists usually need some time to become accustomed to driving on the right. The route from Paris is entirely toll motorway to Alicante.

There are also long-distance ferries between Plymouth and Santander (a 24-hour trip). From Santander follow the N623 to Madrid then the N111 to Valencia or Alicante, or the N240 from Santander to Barcelona.

Car ferries link Ibiza regularly with Barcelona, Alicante and Valencia, as well as with Palma de Mallorca. Reservations for vehicle space may be difficult in the high season so book far in advance.

By bus: Express coach services operate between London and Barcelona and the Costa Blanca, with frequent departures in summer. You can travel by coach as part of a package holiday from London.

BY RAIL: There are two main routes to Spain: via Paris and Barcelona (27 hours) and Paris and Madrid (32 hours). Connections can then be made to Valencia and Alicante. Couchettes and sleepers are available, and you should book at least two weeks in advance for trips in peak periods. Besides the first- and second-class fares, the Inter-Rail Card may be used in Spain by travellers under 26, women over 60 and men over 65. Another fare, the Transalpino, for those under 26 is also a bargain.

Eurailpass: North Americans—in fact, anyone except residents of Europe—can travel on a flat-rate, unlimited mileage ticket valid for first-class rail travel anywhere in Western Europe outside of Great Britain. The price depends on whether you want to travel for two weeks or longer, up to three months. But you must sign up before you leave home.

Student-railpass: It's the same system but it buys second-class accommodation at a cheaper price. Only full-time students under 26 are eligible.

From North America

Many daily connecting flights are offered between approximately a dozen large American cities and Ibiza (via Madrid or Barcelona). In addition, daily connections are available between Ibiza and Montreal, Ottawa, Toronto, Quebec and Vancouver.

The bargain-conscious tourist has several choices:

- The 14- to 45-day **Excursion Fare** may be booked and ticketed at any time. This fare is not subject to any cancellation fees, but does change in price according to season of travel.

- The **APEX** fare must be booked and paid for 21 days prior to departure and is subject to a cancellation penalty unless you have a medical certificate. The ticket is good from 7 to 120 days and no stop-overs are permitted.

- **"Visit Spain"** fares are low-priced and let you visit several Spanish cities during 45 days at a flat rate. However, you're allowed to come back to the same city twice only for connections. This fare includes the Balearic Islands.

- **Executive Fares** offer extra service and attention during flights for the price of a one-way ticket plus a small extra charge. Stop-overs are permitted.

Charter Flights and Package Tours are available through airlines and travel agents. You'll also find charter flights organized by private organizations, companies or church groups.

The ITX (Inclusive Tour Excursion) lets you book only 7 days ahead for your 7- to 45-day stay. You can prolong your stay by up to 45 days for a reasonable fee. There's also an added fee if you plan additional stops.

When to Go

Ibiza is blessed with a relatively mild climate throughout the year. Maximum temperatures in winter, however, can be a bit cooler than in many other Spanish resorts.

Even in the summer months when the weather is at its warmest, the nights can turn chilly, so it's best to go prepared with a sweater or light jacket.

Similarly, though rain is the exception rather than the rule in the summer, it can catch visitors unaware. A pack-away raincoat or umbrella is a good investment.

During the year Ibiza enjoys an average of 300 days of sunshine with a daily mean of five hours in winter and more than ten hours a day in summer. Humidity is stable, remaining about 70 per cent throughout the year.

Because the winter climate can be somewhat unpredictable, package tours during this season are cheaper than in the summer, and you'll find the resorts much quieter though service can suffer as a result.

The chart below, showing average 24-hour temperatures as well as rainy and sunny days by month, may help you plan your wardrobe for Ibiza.

	J	F	M	A	M	J	J	A	S	O	N	D
Air temperature												
F	54	53	56	59	63	71	77	79	72	68	61	56
C	12	12	13	15	17	22	25	26	22	20	16	13
Water temperature												
F	56	57	57	61	67	71	76	80	73	68	65	61
C	13	14	14	16	16	21	24	26	22	20	18	16
Days of sunshine	26	14	21	15	28	28	27	31	28	19	24	28

All figures shown are approximate monthly averages.

Planning Your Budget

To give you a idea of what to expect, here are some average prices in Spanish pesetas. However, all prices must be regarded as approximate, as inflation creeps relentlessly up.

Airport transfer. Bus to the centre to Ibiza Town 30 ptas., taxi 500 ptas.

Babysitters. 300 ptas. per hour before midnight, 350 ptas. after midnight.

Bicycle and moped hire. Bicycle 150 ptas. per day, moped 650 ptas. per day, motorscooter 1,000 ptas. per day.

Buses (one way). Ibiza to Santa Eulalia 50 ptas., to San Antonio 45 ptas., to San Miguel 55 ptas.

Camping. 175–225 ptas. per person per day, 160–250 ptas. per tent per day.

Car hire (unlimited mileage). *Seat 127* 2,400 ptas. per day, 14,200 ptas. per week. *Ford Fiesta* 3,200 ptas. per day, 19,000 ptas. per week. *Seat 131* 4,300 ptas. per day, 27,000 ptas. per week. Add 3% tax.

Cigarettes (per packet of 20). Spanish brands 35–75 ptas., imported 135–180 ptas.

Entertainment. Bullfight, *sol* 1,400 ptas., *sombra* 1,600 ptas. Casino 400 ptas. Discotheque 800–1,500 ptas.

Excursions. Santa Gertrudis burro ranch 775 ptas., Espalmador organized boat excursion 1,700 ptas., Formentera boat trip 300 ptas.

Hairdressers. *Woman's* haircut 1,000–1,500 ptas., shampoo and set 600–800 ptas., permanent wave 2,000–2,500 ptas. *Man's* haircut 350 ptas.

Hotels (double room with bath in season). ******** 4,200–5,100 ptas., ******* 1,625–3,500 ptas., ****** 1,200–2,200 ptas., ***** 1,000–2,000 ptas.

Meals and drinks. Continental breakfast 175 ptas. lunch/dinner 600–1,800 ptas., beer 60–100 ptas., coffee 45–100 ptas., soft drinks 75 ptas., Spanish brandy 60–150 ptas., *sangría* (carafe) 300–350 ptas.

Shopping bag. Bread (500 g.) 40 ptas., butter (180 g.) 170 ptas., 6 eggs 55–70 ptas., beefsteak (500 g.) 360–400 ptas., instant coffee (200 g.) 480 ptas., wine (litre) 150–300 ptas., fruit juice (litre) 115 ptas.

Sports. *Golf* green fee 1,000 ptas. per day, lesson 1,200 ptas. per hour. *Horseriding* 600 ptas. per hour. *Tennis* 300 ptas. per hour, lesson 800 ptas. per hour, membership card 1,500 ptas. per month.

Taxi. 24 ptas. per km. (road), 30 ptas. per km. (town), waiting charge 600 ptas. per hour.

BLUEPRINT for a Perfect Trip

An A-Z Summary of Practical Information and Facts

Contents

A star (*) following an entry indicates that relevant prices are to be found on page 99. Listed after most main entries is an appropriate Spanish translation, usually in the singular. You'll find this vocabulary useful when asking for assistance.

AIRPORT* *(aeropuerto)*.

Ibiza's modern terminal serves both international and domestic flights. Porters are always available to carry your bags the few steps to the taxi rank or bus-stop. Souvenir shops, tourist information offices, car hire and currency-exchange counters operate here, as well as a duty free shop. Ordinary shops in the towns sell perfume, tobacco and alcohol, tax included, at reasonable prices. Airline buses link the airport with the centre of Ibiza Town, a 15-minute drive. There is a bus service every 30 minutes.

Porter!	**¡Mozo!**
Taxi!	**¡Taxi!**
Where's the bus for…?	**¿Dónde está el autobús para…?**

BABYSITTERS* *(señorita para cuidar niños)*.

The bigger hotels organize this as a matter of course. Prices depend on the time of the day and the length of the engagement.

Can you get me a babysitter for tonight?	**¿Puede conseguirme una señorita para cuidar los niños esta noche?**

BICYCLE and MOTORSCOOTER HIRE* *(bicicletas/scooters de alquiler)*.

A practical, fun way to explore the islands is to hire two-wheeled transportation capable of getting you over the most narrow, bumpy paths. Bicycles may often be hired at the same places that rent out motorscooters and mopeds but at about one-quarter the price. A driving licence is required when renting a vespa or a mobylette.

Vespas are squat motorscooters of 150 to 175 cc., powerful enough to transport driver and passenger with ease.

Mobylettes are more elementary, 49-cc. mopeds requiring little mechanical knowledge; passengers are not permitted. Maximum speed is about 20 miles per hour.

B   For more adventurous speedsters, *Bultaco* trail bikes (250 cc.) are occasionally available.

The use of crash helmets is compulsory in Spain when driving a motorcycle, whatever the capacity of the engine.

I'd like to hire a bicycle.	**Quisiera alquilar una bicicleta.**
What's the charge per day/week?	**¿Cuánto cobran por día/semana?**

BOAT SERVICES. Modern ferries link Ibiza with Barcelona. Valencia, Alicante and Mallorca all year round. The direct crossing between Barcelona and Ibiza takes about 10 hours; between Alicante and Ibiza, 7. The trip from Mallorca to Ibiza takes 5 hours. Cabins and berths are available on the overnight boat. During the summer, reservations for your car should be made in advance.

Getting to Formentera is quick and easy from Ibiza. Motorboats ply between the two islands in an hour. There are also numerous boat excursions around Ibiza itself that you can find out about on the spot.

The frequency of boat services increases considerably in high season (July 1 to September 30). You can get more detailed information by contacting your travel agent.

BUS SERVICES. On Ibiza the bus service hasn't quite caught up with the tourist boom. However, tickets are cheap, and the crowding just might go under the heading of local colour. Private companies link Ibiza with both San Antonio and Santa Eulalia as well as northern towns. They also operate local runs to beaches. The main lines run a bus every half hour during summer and sometimes extra ones during rush periods. Even so, tourists have been known to miss the last bus. Note that there's no east-west bus service across the island. To get from San Antonio to Santa Eulalia you must change in Ibiza Town. This jaunt takes about 90 minutes. A hitch-hiker could do it in 20 minutes if he's lucky.

When's the next bus to…?	**¿Cuándo sale el próximo autobús para…?**
single (one-way)	**ida**
return (round-trip)	**ida y vuelta**

C   **CAMPING**★ *(camping).* Although hotels have been sprouting like mushrooms, camping has been somewhat neglected on Ibiza. Sites are located near San Antonio (off Ibiza Town road), at Cala Bassa, Punta Arabí and Cala de Portinatx. You can also camp at sites near Santa Eulalia (Playa de es Canar) and Ibiza Town (Playa d'en Bossa). Less demanding wanderers have been known to set up camp in Ibiza's coastal caves. If you sleep out in the open, don't stay too close to camping and caravan (trailer) sites. Police responsible for the campsite may awaken you to check identity.

On Formentera camping is prohibited.

May we camp here?	**¿Podemos acampar aquí?**
We've a tent/caravan (trailer).	**Tenemos una tienda de camping/ una caravana.**

CAR HIRE* *(coches de alquiler).* Car hire firms in Ibiza handle a wide variety of cars, from the humble Seat 133 to more expensive Chryslers and Mercedes. The rates vary accordingly and those given on page 99 are sample prices of major operators.

Off-season rates are about 20% lower. General conditions include a refundable deposit plus 20% of the estimated rental charge paid in advance. (Holders of major credit cards are normally exempt from deposits and advance payment.) There's also a 3% traffic tax on total rental charges. Third-party insurance is automatically included; for an extra fee the customer may have full insurance coverage. Renting a car for the day usually means from 8 a.m. to 8 p.m. Fuel (and traffic fines) are the customer's responsibility. In principle, you're supposed to have a current International Driving Licence. In practice, British, American and European licences are accepted almost everywhere.

I'd like to rent a car tomorrow.	**Quisiera alquilar un coche para mañana.**
for one day/a week	**por un día/una semana**
Please include full insurance.	**Haga el favor de incluir el seguro todo riesgo.**

CATERING *(abastecedor).* If you've a holiday villa or apartment and want someone to organize anything from a small reception to a complete dinner, inquire at the Ibiza tourist office for the name of a caterer.

I want to give a… for 10 guests.	**Quiero dar un/una … para 10 invitados.**
cocktail party/small dinner party	**aperitivo/pequeña cena**

C **CIGARETTES, CIGARS, TOBACCO⋆** *(cigarrillos, puros, tabaco).* Most Spanish cigarettes are made of strong, black tobacco. They're sold in packets of 20, with or without filter. One of the most popular Spanish brands is *Ducados.* Nearly all major foreign cigarettes are available at two to three times the price of local ones. There are a few Spanish-brand cigarettes of light tobacco at reasonable prices, such as *Un-X-Dos* (filter) and *Bisonte* (non-filter). The government tobacco monopoly operates one or more tobacco shop in each town; incidentally, postage stamps may also be purchased there.

Spanish cigars are passable and cheap. Cuban cigars are available and are a real bargain.

Spanish pipe tobacco is considered by most foreigners to be a bit on the rough side.

A packet of cigarettes/matches.	**Un paquete de cigarrillos/cerillas.**
filter-tipped	**con filtro**
without filter	**sin filtro**
light tobacco	**tabaco rubio**
dark tobacco	**tabaco negro**

CLOTHING. Considering Ibiza's reputation for freewheeling tolerance, it would be surprising if anyone laid down rules. Dress is quite informal, ranging from discreet to outlandish. As everywhere else, good taste is the ultimate rule.

When you're packing, don't fail to consider the calendar. In July and August you're unlikely to need anything beyond the lightest summer clothing, day or night. But any other time of year—even when it's blistering hot at midday—you may have to dress warmer for cool night breezes. Cotton is preferable to synthetic fabrics in the hot weather.

On the beach dressing poses less of a problem. Some people wear nothing at all (there's official nude bathing in certain areas) and many women go topless.

When you're walking to or from the beach, shirts or informal dresses are recommended to be worn over swimsuits; the same goes for town-wear. More sober clothing should, as a matter of courtesy, be worn when visiting churches. Don't put on a swimsuit or shorts, for example.

When buying shoes or clothing, the following conversion table should be useful (remember though that sizes vary somewhat according to manufacturers):

C

Women								
Clothing			Shirts			Shoes		
GB	USA	Spain	GB	USA	Spain	GB	USA	Spain
10	8	40	32	10	38	3	4½	35
12	10	42	34	12	40	4	5½	36
14	12	44	36	14	42	5	6½	37
16	14	46	38	16	44	6	7½	38
18	16	48	40	18	46	7	8½	39

Men							
Clothing		Shirts		Shoes			
GB / USA	Spain	GB / USA	Spain	GB	USA	Spain	
36	46	14	36	6	6½	40	
38	48	14½	37	7	7½	41	
40	50	15	38	8	8½	42	
42	52	15½	39	9	9½	43	
44	54	16	40	10	10½	44	

COMMUNICATIONS

Post Offices (correos): See also under HOURS. Post offices are for mail and telegrams only; you can't usually make telephone calls from here. Some of them limit acceptance of registered mail to certain times, and they often stay open a few hours after the normal closing for telegraph business. So, if the man won't sell you stamps then, don't be angry. In fact you can avoid the crowds and buy stamps (sello) at any tobacconist's (tabacos).

Mail boxes are yellow with red stripes.

Parcels (paquete) up to to two kilos (4.4 lbs.) can be mailed from local post offices. Heavier parcels must be sent from the main post office in Ibiza.

C   If you don't know ahead of time where you'll be staying, you can have your mail addressed to *lista de correos* (poste restante or general delivery) at whichever town is most convenient:

> Mr. John Smith
> Lista de Correos
> San Antonio Abad
> Ibiza (Baleares), Spain

Take your passport with you to the post office for identification.

Telegrams *(telegramas):* The main post office in Ibiza Town handles telegrams from 9 a.m. to 1.30 p.m. and 3 to 8 p.m. daily, branches from 9 a.m. to 2 p.m. only. Your hotel desk will also take care of telegrams for you.

Night-letters or night-rate telegrams *(telegrama de noche)* are delivered the following morning and cost less than straight-rate messages.

Telephones *(teléfono):* Ibiza's automatic dialling system allows you to dial numbers throughout Spain. However, it's often impossible to reach a number across town. Many bars and restaurants have a pay telephone. Coins of 5, 25 and 50 pesetas should be lined up on the ledge before dialling. Unused coins will be returned.

For overseas calls, consult your hotel switchboard operator or go to the telephone office in the nearest town. (There are no telephone offices on Formentera.) You may also use certain call boxes in the street, marked *interurbanes* or *internacionales*. Be sure to have enough change to complete your call, as these public telephones have no numbers and the other party cannot ring you back. To reverse the charges, ask for *cobro revertido*. For a personal (person to person) call, specify *persona a persona*.

Telephone Spelling Code:

A	Antonio	G	Gerona	M	Madrid	S	Sábado
B	Barcelona	H	Historia	N	Navarro	T	Tarragona
C	Carmen	I	Inés	Ñ	Ñoño	U	Ulises
CH	Chocolate	J	José	O	Oviedo	V	Valencia
D	Dolores	K	Kilo	P	París	W	Washington
E	Enrique	L	Lorenzo	Q	Querido	X	Xiquena
F	Francia	L	Llobregat	R	Ramón	Y	Yegua
						Z	Zaragoza

Have you received any mail for me?	**¿Ha recibido correo para mí?**

A stamp for this letter/postcard, please.	**Por favor, un sello para esta carta/tarjeta.**
express (special delivery)	**urgente**
airmail	**vía aérea**
registered	**certificado**
I want to send a telegram to…	**Quisiera mandar un telegrama a…**
Can you get me this number in…?	**¿Puede comunicarme con este número en…?**

COMPLAINTS *(reclamación).* Tourism is Spain's leading industry, and the government takes complaints from tourists very seriously.

Hotels and restaurants: By law, all hotels and restaurants must maintain a supply of complaint forms *(hoja de reclamaciones)* accessible to guests. The original of this triplicate document should be sent to the regional office of the Ministry of Tourism; one copy stays with the establishment against which the complaint is registered, while the final copy remains in your hands as a record. Merely asking for this is usually enough of a threat to resolve most matters.

Bad merchandise; car repairs: Consumer protection is in its infancy in Spain. If you think you've been taken advantage of, all you can do is appeal to the proprietor.

In the event of gross abuse take your problem to the local tourist office, or the *Guardia Civil.*

CONSULATES *(consulado)*

British vice-consulate*: Avenida Isidoro Macabich, 45, Ibiza; tel. 30 18 18.

Irish consulate: Gran Vía Carlos III, 94, Barcelona; tel. 3 30 96 52.

U.S. consulate: Vía Layetana, 33 Barcelona; tel. 3 19 95 50.

Almost all western European countries have consular offices on Ibiza, Majorca or in Barcelona. All embassies are located in Madrid.

---

* Also for citizens of Commonwealth countries.

C

If you run into trouble with the authorities or the police, consult your consulate for advice.

Where's the British/American consulate?
It's very urgent.

¿Dónde está el consulado británico/americano?
Es muy urgente.

CONVERTER CHARTS. For fluid and distance measures, see page 111. Spain uses the metric system.

Temperature

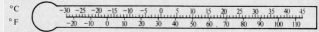

Length

Weight

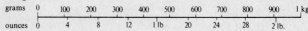

CRIME and THEFT *(crimen; robo).* Unfortunately, even on a small island like Ibiza, there has been an upsurge in petty thievery. In crowded and colourful places like markets, tourists should be on the lookout for pickpockets and bag-snatchers.

I want to report a theft.   **Quiero denunciar un robo.**

CUSTOMS and ENTRY FORMALITIES. Most visitors, including citizens of Great Britain, the U.S.A., Canada and Eire, require only a valid passport—no visa, no health certificate—to enter Spain. Visitors from Australia, New Zealand and South Africa, however, have to have a visa. If in doubt, check with your travel agent before departure.

The formalities at Ibiza airport are generally so informal that passports aren't even stamped. You're usually entitled to stay in Spain for up to 90 days. If you expect to remain longer, a Spanish consulate or tourist office can advise you.

The severely uniformed, white-gloved Spanish customs officials may or may not ask you to open your suitcase for inspection. As in most countries, they work on hunches. Be courteous and try to be honest. If you attempt to deceive them you may regret it.

The following chart shows what main duty-free items you may take into Spain and, when returning home, into your own country:

Into:	Cigarettes		Cigars		Tobacco	Spirits		Wine
Spain*	200 (400)	or	50 (100)	or	250 g. (500)	1 l.	or	2 l.
Australia	200	or	50	or	250 g.	1 l.	or	1 l.
Canada	200	and	50	and	900 g.	1.1 l.	or	1.1 l.
Eire	200	or	50	or	250 g.	1 l.	and	2 l.
N. Zealand	200	or	50	or	½ lb.	1.1 l.	and	1.1 l.
S. Africa	400	and	50	and	250 g.	1 l.	and	1 l.
U.K.	200	or	50	or	250 g.	1 l.	and	2 l.
U.S.A.	200	and	100	and	**	1 l.	or	1 l.

* The figures in parentheses are for non-European visitors only.
** A reasonable quantity.

In addition to personal clothing, jewelry and perfume, you may bring into the country two still cameras with accessories and five rolls of film, a home-movie camera and ten rolls of film, a pair of binoculars and similar items for personal use. For some items you may have to sign a guarantee that you won't sell them while in Spain or you may have to put up a deposit (refundable). While there's no limit for tourists on the importation of foreign currencies or traveller's cheques, non-residents can't bring in more than 100,000 pesetas—which must be declared upon arrival—or leave the country with more than 20,000 pesetas.

I've nothing to declare. **No tengo nada que declarar.**
It's for my personal use. **Es para mi uso personal.**

D DRIVING IN SPAIN

Entering Spain: To bring your car into Spain you will need:

International Driving Licence, or your normal driving licence	car registration papers nationality plate or sticker	Green Card (an extension to your regular insurance policy, making it valid for foreign countries)

Recommended: a Spanish bail bond. If you injure somebody in an accident in Spain, you can be jailed while the accident is being investigated. This bond will bail you out. Apply to your insurance company.

Driving conditions on Ibiza: The rules are the same as in mainland Spain and the rest of the Continent: drive on the right, pass on the left, yield right of way to all vehicles coming from the right. Spanish drivers tend to use their horn when overtaking. If your car has seat belts, it's obligatory to use them; fines for non-compliance are high.

The roads of Ibiza are a few years behind the times. Except for the San Antonio–Ibiza motorway and other main thoroughfares, they're narrow, twisting and filled with pot-holes, badly signposted—actually, delightful providing you drive carefully and are not in a hurry. Be warned that quaint local attractions can become deadly perils on the road—horse-drawn carts, donkeys, sheep, goats and the occasional pedestrian or hitch-hiker. When passing through villages, drive with extra care.

Other hazards to look out for include loose gravel and sand on the roadway. (The latter can be as slippery as ice!) Give plenty of leeway to motorbikes, scooters and bicycles. They drive—justly—as if they were entitled to a generous share of roadway. Never pass any vehicle or obstruction without signalling.

Traffic police: The armed Civil Guard *(Guardia Civil)* patrol the few highways of Ibiza by car and on powerful motorcycles. Always in pairs, these tough-looking *hombres* are courteous and will stop to help anyone in trouble. They're also severe on lawbreakers.

If you receive a fine, you may be expected to pay it on the spot. The most common offenses include passing without directional-indicator lights flashing, travelling too close to the car in front and travelling with a burned-out head- or tail-light. (Spanish law shrewdly requires you to carry a spare bulb at all times.)

Parking: In Ibiza Town, San Antonio and Santa Eulalia, the traffic
police have become very much stricter about incorrect parking, and

cars are either towed away to the police pound (behind Avenida Isidoro Macabich) or a large and heavy yellow metal clamp called a *cepo* is affixed to the rear wheel of the car, thereby immobilizing it. To remove the clamp, a special key is needed, and as there appears to be only one police jeep equipped with the key, a motorist may find himself having to wait up to 24 hours before becoming mobile again. In the case of the *cepo*, a notice is placed on the windscreen warning the motorist not to drive as irreparable damage may occur to the car. In the case of both the *cepo* and towing away, a fine must be paid.

Fuel and oil: All fuel is sold through the government monopoly, Campsa. It's theoretically available in three grades—90, 96, and 98 octane—but not every station has a choice of fuels at a given time. For the sake of your car, buy only the best grade available. Service stations are still scarce on the island so you may have to queue up when you find one. Petrol station hours are completely irregular at weekends and during fiestas (see *Diario de Ibiza* for a listing of stations remaining open), and a motorist may have to go from Santa Eulalia to San Jose for petrol on a Sunday. Therefore, the local rule is: always fill up on a Friday and before a fiesta. Also before nightfall in the summer, when usually only one station is open on the whole island.

Fluid measures

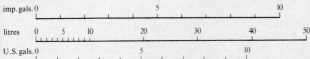

Distance

Breakdowns: Because of the heavy workload and a shortage of qualified mechanics, repairs may take longer than they would at home. Spare parts are readily available for Spanish-built cars, but the spares of other makes may be very difficult to obtain.

Road signs: Most road signs are the standard pictographs used throughout Europe. However, you may encounter these written signs:

Aparcamiento	Parking
Atención	Caution
Baches	Pot-holes

D

Blandones	Soft shoulders
Bordes deteriorados	Deteriorated road edges
Ceda el paso	Give way (Yield)
Despacio	Slow
Desviación	Diversion (Detour)
Escuela	School
Estacionamento prohibido	No parking
Obras	Road works
¡Pare!	Stop
Peatones	Pedestrians
Peligro	Danger
Salida de camiones	Lorry (Truck) exit

(International) Driving Licence	**carné de conducir (internacional)**
car registration papers	**permiso de circulación**
Green Card	**carta verde**

Are we on the right road for…?	**¿Es ésta la carretera hacia…?**
Fill the tank please, top grade.	**Llénelo, por favor, con super.**
Check the oil/tires/battery.	**Por favor, controle el aceite/los neumáticos/la batería.**

I've had a breakdown.	**Mi coche se ha estropeado.**
There's been an accident.	**Ha habido un accidente.**

DRUGS. Although Ibiza has achieved a reputation as a free and easy centre of the drug scene, the Spanish police have no sympathy for narcotics of any sort or their users here or on the mainland. Sentences can range from six months to 20 years.

E **ELECTRIC CURRENT** *(corriente eléctrica)*. Both 125- and 220-volt, 50 c., A.C., exists on the island. To play it safe, ask at your hotel desk.

Occasionally, especially when it rains, all the electricity goes out for a short time. No one has explained why, but some think it adds to the island's romantic mood. Most hotels supply a candle in every room.

If you have trouble with any of your appliances, ask your desk-clerk to recommend an *electricista*.

What's the voltage—125 or 220?	**¿Cuál es el voltaje—ciento veinticinco (125) o doscientos veinte (220)?**
an adaptor	**un adaptador**
a battery	**una pila**

112

EMERGENCIES *(urgencia)*. If your hotel desk-clerk isn't handy to help, here are a couple of pertinent telephone numbers:

Police Emergency: 091   Ambulance: 30 12 14   Fire: 30 11 01

Depending on the nature of the emergency, refer to the separate entries in this section such as CONSULATES, HEALTH AND MEDICAL CARE, POLICE, etc.

GUIDES and INTERPRETERS *(guía, intérprete).* Local tourist offices can direct you to qualified guides and interpreters and will also inform you of the prices generally asked for.

In most centres, an English-speaking guide can be hired at short notice.

We'd like an English-speaking guide.	**Queremos un guía que hable inglés.**
I need an English interpreter.	**Necesito un intérprete de inglés.**

HAGGLING. Don't confuse the shops of Ibiza and Formentera with the bazaars of the Middle East. Merchants mark their prices and almost without exception stick by them. Bargaining might be pointless as well as tasteless—except perhaps with hippy vendors.

HAIRDRESSERS*. Prices vary widely according to the class of the establishment, but rates are often displayed in the window. Most hairdressers include a service charge in the price, but it is customary to give an additional tip of 5 to 10%. Men's barbers are called *barbería*, women's salons, *peluquería.*

The following vocabulary will help:

I'd like a shampoo and set.	**Quiero lavado y marcado.**
I want a...	**Quiero...**
haircut	**un corte de pelo**
razor cut	**un corte a navaja**
blow-dry (brushing)	**un modelado**
permanent wave	**una permanente**
color rinse/hair dye	**un reflejo/un tinte**
manicure	**una manicura**
Don't cut it too short.	**No me lo corte mucho.**
A little more off (here).	**Un poco más (aquí).**

H **HEALTH and MEDICAL CARE.** With Ibiza's climate and adequate standards of hygiene, most tourists who suffer illness have only themselves to blame. Too much sun, food or alcohol—more likely a combination of all three—have ruined many a holiday. The motto is moderation.

To be completely at ease, make certain your health-insurance policy covers any illness or accident while on holiday. Your travel agent can also fix you up with Spanish tourist insurance *(ASTES)*, but it is a slow-moving process. *ASTES* covers doctor's fees and clinical care in the event of accident or illness.

Do your eyes a favour and wear sunglasses. You may never have seen the sun so brightly and glaringly reflected off white walls.

There are doctors in the towns on Ibiza, and their consulting hours are posted. For less serious matters, first-aid personnel, called *practicantes,* may be consulted. Some *practicantes* make daily rounds of the major tourist hotels, just in case.

Hospitals: There are a number of out-patient clinics on the island, one of them operated round the clock in Ibiza Town. In case of grave emergency, your hotel staff would probably send you there.

Pharmacies: Drugstores *(farmacias),* are usually open during shopping hours. After hours, one shop in each town is always on duty for emergencies. Its address is posted daily at all the other chemists'.

Water: When Spaniards drink water, it's almost invariably bottled water, rather than from the tap. It's quite common to order water brought to one's room. If you're particularly sensitive to a change in water, watch out, too, for the ice cubes in drinks. Water varies enormously in taste and quality, and the bottled variety is good, clean and cheap.

a bottle of...	**una botella de...**
fizzy (carbonated) mineral water/still spring water	**agua mineral gasificada/ agua mineral**
Is this drinking water?	**¿Es esta agua potable?**
a dentist	**un dentista**
a doctor	**un doctor**
an ambulance	**una ambulancia**
hospital	**hospital**
an upset stomach	**molestias de estómago**
sunstroke	**una insolación**
Get a doctor, quickly!	**¡Llamen a un médico, rápidamente!**

HITCH-HIKING *(auto-stop)*. In Spain, hitch-hiking is permitted everywhere.

Can you give us a lift to…?   **¿Puede llevarnos a…?**

HOTELS and ACCOMMODATION* *(hotel; alojamiento)*. Spanish hotel prices are no longer government-controlled. Accommodation in the Balearics ranges from a simple but always clean room in a *pensión* (boarding house) to the more luxurious surroundings of a resort hotel. Before the guest takes the room he fills out a form indicating the hotel category, room number, price and signs it. Breakfast is normally included in the room rate.

However, the overwhelming majority of tourists arriving in Ibiza have reserved and paid for their accommodation in advance through package-tour operators abroad. For them the question of officially posted prices is strictly academic. Off-season (see WHEN TO GO, page 98) rates are theoretically lower, and vacancies, of course, are much more numerous.

An increasingly important aspect of Ibiza tourism is a package arrangement consisting of a furnished apartment or villa. The cost is often little more than the scheduled airfare alone. But arrangements usually have to be made well in advance.

Other forms of accommodation

Hotel-Residencia and Hostal: With a few luxurious exceptions, these are modest hotels, often family concerns. They are also graded by stars (one to three). A three-star *hostal* usually costs about the same as a two-star hotel.

Pensión: Boarding house, graded 1 to 3, with few amenities.

Youth hostels: While there aren't any youth hostels on Ibiza or Formentera, penny-wise holidaymakers of any age will easily find other lodging at really low rates. See CAMPING for information.

a single/double room   **una habitación sencilla/doble**
with bath/shower   **con baño/ducha**

What's the rate per night?   **¿Cuál es el precio por noche?**

HOURS. Schedules here revolve around the siesta, one of the really great Spanish discoveries, aimed at keeping people out of the midday

H sun. The word has become universal; unfortunately, the custom hasn't. But when in Spain you should certainly try it.

To accommodate the midday pause most shops and offices are open from 9 a.m. to 1 p.m. and then from 4 to 8 p.m.

Banks generally open from 9 a.m. to 2 p.m., Monday to Friday, till 1 p.m. on Saturday.

Post offices open from 9 a.m. to 2 p.m., Monday to Saturday. The main office in Ibiza Town keeps longer hours, from 9 a.m. to 1.30 and 3 to 8 p.m.

Restaurants start serving lunch about 1 p.m. and dinner—earlier than on the mainland—between 8 and 11 p.m.

L **LANGUAGE.** The official language of Spain, Castilian, is understood everywhere. However, the islanders customarily communicate among themselves in Ibicenco, derived from the Catalan language. Since Spanish is, in effect, not the local language for the residents, they may speak it more slowly than mainland Spaniards do. English and French are useful back-up languages in tourist areas.

On a brief visit to Ibiza it would be impractical to try very hard to speak the local version of Catalan. A much more useful tool is Spanish, understood by practically everyone on the island. But a few words of Ibicenco dialect will go a long way in producing a smile and friendship.

	Ibicenco	Castilian
Good morning	*Bon dia*	*Buenos días*
Good afternoon	*Bones tardes*	*Buenas tardes*
Good night	*Bona nit*	*Buenas noches*
Thank you	*Gràcies*	*Gracias*
You're welcome	*De res*	*De nada*
Please	*Per favor*	*Por favor*
Goodbye	*Adéu*	*A diós*

And everywhere you'll hear an indispensible, all-purpose Spanish expression. Said with a shrug, it can mean anything from "you're welcome" to "who cares?". The phrase is: *es igual.*

The Berlitz phrase book, SPANISH FOR TRAVELLERS, covers most situations you're likely to encounter in your travels in Spain. In addition, the Berlitz Spanish-English/English-Spanish pocket dictionary contains a 12,500 word glossary of each language, plus a menu reader supplement.

LAUNDRY and DRY-CLEANING. Most hotels will handle laundry and dry-cleaning, but they'll usually charge more than a laundry *(lavandería)* or a dry-cleaners *(tintorería)*. You'll find do-it-yourself launderettes in a few areas.

I must have this for tomorrow morning.	**Lo necesito para mañana por la mañana.**

LOST AND FOUND PROPERTY; LOST CHILDREN *(objetos perdidos; niños perdidos).* Check first at your hotel desk. Then report the loss to the municipal police or the *Guardia Civil* (Civil Guard).

Children are much pampered throughout Spain; lost children are never neglected. If a child gets lost on a beach, inquire at the nearest beach bar or restaurant. In towns, a lost child would be delivered to the municipal police station or Civil Guard barracks, which is where you should go if you lose a child—or find one.

I've lost my wallet/handbag.	**He perdido mi cartera/bolso.**

MAPS and STREET NAMES. On Ibiza and Formentera, some places have two names, one Castilian, another Ibicenco—a situation that often puzzles tourists. To add to the confusion, maps aren't always consistent in citing place names. With the upsurge in regional consciousness that followed the death of General Franco, place names have become something of a bone of contention here, as elsewhere in Spain. Some people would like to see all Castilian place names changed to their Ibicenco equivalents. The more strident of them go around the island spray-painting signposts, altering "San Jose", for example, to read "Sant Josip". Within towns and villages the words for "street", "square" and so on have been changed from Castilian to Ibicenco, but there are no plans afoot to re-baptize the streets or squares themselves. However, when new streets are created they are given Ibicenco names.

The maps in this guide were prepared by Falk-Verlag, Hamburg.

a street plan of ...	**un plano de la ciudad de ...**
a road map of the island	**un mapa de carreteras de la isla**

M **MEETING PEOPLE.** The Spanish, as a whole, are one of the world's most open and hospitable people, easy to talk to and approach, generous to a fault. *"Mi casa es tu casa"* is commonly heard—and meant. On the beach, in a bar, at a disco, you'll have no problem getting to know the local people.

A simple *bon dia*—"good morning" or "good day" in the Ibicenco dialect—will go a long way. It should precede any conversation, even if you stop somebody in the street to ask directions or walk into a bar to order a drink. Try *bones tardes* for "good afternoon" or "good evening". Always say *adéu* (goodbye) when you leave.

When, in a restaurant, your neighbour is about to start his meal, wish him *bon profit* ("enjoy your meal").

As for meeting fellow tourists, try participating in organized outings like barbecues, boat rides and the like. Or simply hang out at the hotel pool by day and the disco by night.

MONEY MATTERS

Currency: The monetary unit of Spain is the *peseta* (abbreviated *pta*).
  Coins: 1, 5, 10, 25, 50 and 100 pesetas.
  Banknotes: 100, 500, 1,000 and 5,000 pesetas.
  A 5-peseta coin is traditionally called a *duro*, so if someone should quote a price as 10 duros, he means 50 pesetas. For currency restrictions, see CUSTOMS AND ENTRY FORMALITIES.

Exchange Offices: Outside normal banking hours (see HOURS), many travel agencies and other businesses displaying a *cambio* sign will change foreign currency into pesetas. The exchange rate is a bit less favourable than in the banks. Both banks and exchange offices pay slightly more for traveller's cheques than for cash. Always take your passport with you when you go to change money.

Credit cards: All the internationally recognized cards are accepted by hotels, restaurants and businesses in Spain.

Eurocheques: You'll have no problem settling bills or paying for purchases with Eurocheques.

Traveller's cheques: In tourist areas, shops and all banks, hotels and travel agencies accept them, though you're likely to get a better exchange rate at a national or regional bank. Remember always to take your passport with you if you expect to cash a traveller's cheque.

Paying cash: Although many shops and bars will accept payment in sterling or dollars, you're better off paying in pesetas. Shops will invariably give you less than the bank rate for foreign currency.

Prices: Because of Ibiza's tourist boom—and because it's an island—certain prices tend to be higher than on the mainland of Spain. However, the cost of living remains lower than in many other European countries and North America.

How much your holiday will cost depends upon your budget and taste, but you really don't need a lot of money to have a good time in Spain.

Some prices seem topsy-turvy. In a neigbourhood bar, soft drinks, beer and Spanish brandy all cost about the same. A bottle of mineral water may cost more than a bottle of wine. But, generally, the biggest bargains are in the realm of eating, drinking and smoking.

Where's the nearest bank/ currency exchange office?	**¿Dónde está el banco/la oficina de cambio más cercana?**
I want to change some pounds/ dollars.	**Quiero cambiar libras/dólares**
Do you accept traveller's cheques?	**¿Acepta usted cheques de viaje?**
Can I pay with this credit card?	**¿Puedo pagar con esta tarjeta de crédito?**
How much is that?	**¿Cuánto es?**

NEWSPAPERS and MAGAZINES *(periódico; revista).* During the height of the tourist season, all major British and Continental newspapers are on sale in Ibiza on the evening of their publication day or the following morning. U.S. magazines are available, as well as the Paris-based *International Herald Tribune.*

National magazines of Europe and the United States are also available in great variety.

As for local publications, a weekly, *Ibiza News*, aims at English-speaking tourists.

If you can read a bit of Spanish, *Diario de Ibiza,* the local tabloid daily, will illustrate more than one meaning of the word "insular".

Have you any English-language newspapers?	**¿Tienen periódicos en inglés?**

P **PETS** *(animal doméstico)*. If you want to take your pet dog or cat along to Spain, you'll need a health and rabies inoculation certificate for the animal, stamped by the Spanish consulate in your own country.

In case of need, there is a vet on the island who specializes in domestic pets. Many hotels don't allow pets, so inquire in advance.

Returning to Great Britain or Eire, your pet will have to go through six months of quarantine for having spent time in a country that is not rabies-free. Both the U.S. and Canada reserve the right to impose quarantine.

PHOTOGRAPHY. Beware of lighting situations you may never before have encountered—especially the blinding reflections from the sea and white buildings. You may not be able to trust the electric eye on your automatic camera in these situations. The secret is to compensate for the reflections with a faster shutter speed. Read your instruction book carefully or, before leaving home, talk over the problem with your camera dealer.

Most of the popular film brands and sizes are available on Ibiza but they generally cost more than at home. Local shops promise 24- to 48-hour service for black-and-white as well as colour processing. Add a pinch of salt to the promise.

The Spanish films, *Negra* and *Valca* in black and white, and *Negra-color* in colour, are of good quality and cheaper than the internationally known brands.

I'd like a film for this camera.	**Quisiera un carrete para esta máquina.**
a black-and-white film	**un carrete en blanco y negro**
a colour-slide film	**un carrete de diapositivas**
35-mm film	**carrete de 35 milímetros**
super-8	**super ocho**
How long will it take to develop (and print) this film?	**¿Cuánto tardará en revelar (y sacar copias de) este carrete?**
May I take a picture?	**¿Puedo sacar una fotografía?**

POLICE *(policía)*. There are three police forces in Spain. The most famous, and best recognized, are the *Guardia Civil* (Civil Guard) who wear those distinctive patent-leather hats. Each sizeable town also has

Policía Municipal (municipal police), dressed in blue or grey uniforms with badges. The third unit, the *Policía Nacional* (national police), a national anti-crime unit, can be recognized by their brown uniforms. Actually, all three forces are armed.

If you need police assistance, you can call on any one of the three. Spanish police are efficient, strict and courteous to foreign visitors.

Where's the nearest police station?	**¿Dónde está la comisaría más cercana?**

PUBLIC HOLIDAYS *(fiesta)*

January 1	*Año Nuevo*	New Year's Day
January 6	*Reyes (Epifanía)*	Epiphany
March 19	*San José*	St. Joseph's Day
May 1	*Día del Trabajo*	Labour Day
July 25	*Santiago Apóstol*	St. James' Day
August 15	*Asunción*	Assumption
October 12	*Día de la Hispanidad*	Discovery of America Day (Colombus Day)
November 1	*Todos los Santos*	All Saints' Day
December 8	*Inmaculada Concepción*	Immaculate Conception
December 25	*Navidad*	Christmas Day
Movable dates:	*Viernes Santo*	Good Friday
	Lunes de Pascua	Easter Monday
	Corpus Christi	Corpus Christi

These are only the national holidays of Spain. So many religious, civic or apparently irrelevant holidays are celebrated on Ibiza that nearly every tourist's fortnight is bound to include one. It may be only a formality, with banks and most shops closed for the day. With luck, you may be able to help celebrate one of the more colourful local occasions. Since nearly every town is named after a saint, the saint's days are local fiestas in the respective localities. Ibiza Town lacks a saint's name but not a patron. On August 5, they celebrate the feast day of Our Lady of the Snows. See page 72 for details of some *fiestas* which take place in different parts of Ibiza or Formentera.

Are you open tomorrow?	**¿Está abierto mañana?**

R **RADIO and TV** *(radio; televisión)*. Most hotels have television lounges where you can watch programmes of the two Spanish channels. All programmes are in Spanish..

Travellers with short-wave radios will be able to pick up the BBC World Service and the Voice of America very clearly at night and in the early morning hours. Ibiza's local commercial radio station broadcasts during the daytime only, in the Spanish language, except for very occasional programmes in Ibicenco.

RELIGIOUS SERVICES *(servicio religioso)*. The national religion of Spain is Roman Catholic. On Ibiza, masses are said in no fewer than 33 different Catholic churches, many of them historic edifices. In summer, notices of masses in foreign languages are posted outside major churches in San Antonio and Santa Eulalia.

Protestant services are held from time to time. An Anglican rite is conducted in the Catholic church at San Antonio at 11 a.m. on the first Tuesday of each month. The churches in San Antonio and San Carlos are the most commonly chosen for ecumenical cooperation. Notices may be found on the bulletin boards in hotels and cafés.

There's no Jewish congregation on Ibiza.

What time is mass/the service? **¿A qué hora es la misa/el culto?**
Is it in English? **¿Es en inglés?**

S **SHOE-SHINES** *(limpiabotas)*. In your hotel there'll be a set price for shoe-shining. Itinerant shoe-shine boys seem to be a dying breed on the island. Most people go to Salón Limpiabotas on the corner of Calle Conde Rosellón under the city walls.

Will you clean these shoes, **¿Puede limpiar estos zapatos,**
please? **por favor?**

T **TAXIS*** *(taxi)*. The letters *SP* on the front and rear bumpers of a car don't stand for Spain; they mean *servicio público*. The car is a taxi. It may also have a green light in the front window and a taxi sign. Whatever it looks like, it's a reasonably economical mode of transport by Western standards. Ibiza's taxis have no meters.

The major towns have taxi ranks where the taxis, not the customers, have to queue up most of the time.

122 What's the fare to... **¿Cuánto es la tarifa a...?**

TIME DIFFERENCES. Ibiza sets it clocks to Spanish time which is the same as nearly all countries in Western Europe—Greenwich Mean Time plus one hour. In winter, Spanish clocks are turned back one hour. If your country does the same, the time difference remains the same as in summer.

Punctuality isn't a Spanish—or Ibicenco—virtue. They say the only function that ever starts on time is the bullfight and only because the *toreros* go through agonies if they're delayed.

Los Angeles	Chicago	New York	London	**Ibiza**
3 a.m.	5 a.m.	6 a.m.	11 a.m.	**noon**

What time is it?   **¿Qué hora es?**

TIPPING. Since a service charge is normally included in hotel and restaurant bills, tipping is not obligatory. However, it's appropriate to tip bellboys, filling-station attendants, bullfight ushers, etc., for their service.

The chart below gives some suggestions as to what to leave.

Porter, per bag	35 ptas.
Maid, per week	150 ptas.
Lavatory attendant	10–15 ptas.
Waiter	5–10% (optional)
Taxi driver	10%
Hairdresser/Barber	10%
Tourist guide	10%

TOILETS. There are many expressions for toilets in Spanish: *aseos*, *servicios*, *W.C.*, *water* and *retretes;* the first two terms are the more common.

Public conveniences are as rare as snowstorms on Ibiza. However, just about every bar and restaurant has a toilet for public use. It would be considered polite to buy a cup of coffee or a glass of wine if you drop in specifically to use the facilities.

Where are the toilets?   **¿Dónde están los servicios?**   **123**

T **TOURIST INFORMATION OFFICES** *(oficina de turismo).* Spanish National Tourist Offices are maintained in many countries throughout the world:

British Isles: 57, St. James's St. London S.W. 1, tel. (01) 499–1095.

U.S.A.: 845 N. Michigan Ave., Chicago, Ill. 60611; tel. (312) 944-0215
665 5th Ave., New York, N.Y. 10017; tel. (212) 759-8822
Casa del Hidalgo, Hypolita & St. George streets, St. Augustine, Fla. 32084; tel. (904) 829-6460
1 Hallidie Plaza, Suite 801, San Francisco, CA 94102; tel. (415) 346-8100
Fortaleza 367, P.O. Box 463, San Juan, P.R. 00902; tel. 725-0625

Canada: 60 Bloor St. West, Suite 201, Toronto, Ont. M4W-3B8; tel. (416) 961-3131

These offices will supply you with a wide range of colourful and informative brochures and maps in English on the various towns and regions in Spain. They will also let you consult a copy of the master directory of hotels in Spain, listing all facilities and prices.

Ibiza has a tourist information office at 13, Vara de Rey, Ibiza Town; telephone 30 19 00. Open from 8.30 a.m. to 1 p.m., Monday to Friday; 8.30 a.m. to noon on Saturdays.

Where's the tourist office? **¿Dónde está la oficina de turismo?**

NUMBERS

0	cero	12	doce	31	treinta y uno
1	uno	13	trece	32	treinta y dos
2	dos	14	catorce	40	cuarenta
3	tres	15	quince	50	cincuenta
4	cuatro	16	dieciséis	60	sesenta
5	cinco	17	diecisiete	70	setenta
6	seis	18	dieciocho	80	ochenta
7	siete	19	diecinueve	90	noventa
8	ocho	20	veinte	100	cien
9	nueve	21	veintiuno	101	ciento uno
10	diez	22	veintidós	500	quinientos
11	once	30	treinta	1,000	mil

SOME USEFUL EXPRESSIONS

yes/no	**sí/no**
please/thank you	**por favor/gracias**
excuse me/you're welcome	**perdone/de nada**
where/when/how	**dónde/cuándo/cómo**
how long/how far	**cuánto tiempo/a qué distancia**
yesterday/today/tomorrow	**ayer/hoy/mañana**
day/week/month/year	**día/semana/mes/año**
left/right	**izquierda/derecha**
up/down	**arriba/abajo**
good/bad	**bueno/malo**
big/small	**grande/pequeño**
cheap/expensive	**barato/caro**
hot/cold	**caliente/frío**
old/new	**viejo/nuevo**
open/closed	**abierto/cerrado**
here/there	**aquí/allí**
free (vacant)/occupied	**libre/ocupado**
early/late	**temprano/tarde**
easy/difficult	**fácil/difícil**
Does anyone here speak English?	**¿Hay alguien aquí que hable inglés?**
What does this mean?	**¿Qué quiere decir esto?**
I don't understand.	**No comprendo.**
Please write it down.	**Por favor, escríbalo.**
Is there an admission charge?	**¿Se debe pagar la entrada?**
Waiter!/Waitress!	**¡Camarero!/¡Camarera!**
I'd like…	**Quisiera…**
How much is that?	**¿Cuánto es?**
Have you something less expensive?	**¿Tiene algo más barato?**
Just a minute.	**Un momento.**
Help me, please.	**Ayúdeme, por favor.**
Get a doctor, quickly!	**¡Llamen a un médico, rápidamente!**

125

Index

An asterisk (*) next to a page number indicates a map reference. For index to Practical Information, see page 100.

108/312 RPC